SECRETS OF
Prayer

SELECTIONS FROM
THE WRITINGS OF
ANDREW
MURRAY

BARBOUR
PUBLISHING, INC.
Uhrichsville, Ohio

SECRETS OF
Prayer

© 2000 by Barbour Publishing, Inc.

ISBN 1-58660-032-X

Published by Barbour Publishing, Inc., P.O. Box 719, Uhrichsville, OH 44683 http://www.barbourbooks.com

Member of the
Evangelical Christian
Publishers Association

Printed in the United States of America.

INTRODUCTION

For years, South African pastor and theologian Andrew Murray has been known as an expert writer on the subject of prayer. Now, in this one concise volume, you can benefit from his wisdom.

Secrets of Prayer has been carefully compiled from many of Andrew Murray's books about prayer, including *The Inner Life, The Prayer Life,* and *The Ministry of Intercession.* This collection is short enough to be read in one sitting—but its layout also lends itself to use as a daily devotional. Each selection includes three items: a Scripture passage, a brief prayer, and the insights of Andrew Murray. The language of the text has been updated for ease of reading, while maintaining Murray's treasured insights on the deeper spiritual life.

If you've been seeking a better prayer life, this book may be the key. Let *Secrets of Prayer* guide you toward a closer, more meaningful communion with God.

WAIT UPON GOD

He [Daniel] prayed three times a day,
just as he had always done, giving thanks to his God.
DANIEL 6:10

The more I think of and pray about the religious situation in our country, the deeper my conviction becomes that Christians do not realize that the aim of conversion is to bring them into daily fellowship with the Father in heaven.

For the believer, taking time each day with God's Word and in prayer is indispensable. Each day we need to wait upon God for His presence and His love to be revealed.

It is not enough at conversion to accept forgiveness of sins or even to surrender to God. That is only a beginning. We must understand that we have no power on our own to maintain our spiritual life. We need to receive daily new grace from heaven through fellowship with the Lord Jesus. This cannot be obtained by a hasty prayer or a superficial reading of a few verses from God's Word. We must take time to come into God's presence, to feel our weakness and our need, and to wait on God through His Holy Spirit to renew our fellowship with Him. Then we may expect to be kept by the power of Christ throughout the day.

It is my aim to help Christians to see the absolute necessity of spending time with the Lord Jesus. Without this, the joy and power of God's Holy Spirit in daily life cannot be experienced.

Lord God, as I begin this new year, teach me to know You in deeper prayer fellowship. You have many things to reveal to me. In Jesus' name I ask You to make me a good learner. Amen.

ALONE WITH GOD

"When you pray, go away by yourself,
shut the door behind you,
and pray to your Father secretly."
MATTHEW 6:6

Have you ever thought what a wonderful privilege it is to have the liberty of asking God to meet with you and to hear what you have to say? We should use such a privilege gladly and faithfully.

"When you pray," says Jesus, "go away by yourself, shut the door behind you, and pray to your Father secretly." This means two things. (1) Shut the world out; withdraw from all the thoughts and concerns of the day. (2) Shut yourself in alone with God to pray in secret. Let this be your chief object in prayer, to realize the presence of your heavenly Father. Let your goal be: "Alone with God."

Being alone in His presence and praying to the Father in secret is only the beginning. Come to Him in the full assurance that He knows how you long for His help and guidance. He will listen to you.

Then follows the great promise of verse 6: "Then your Father, who knows all secrets, will reward you." Your Father will see to it that your prayer is not in vain. Prayer in secret will be followed by the secret working of God in my heart.

Lord Jesus, thank You for the promise of Your presence and show me the way to be alone with You. Help me to be childlike and trustful in my fellowship with You, confessing each sin and bringing You my every need. Amen.

THE IMPORTANCE OF FAITH

"Don't be afraid. Just trust me."
MARK 5:36

This is a lesson of the greatest importance. When praying alone in the presence of God, we must trust implicitly in the love of God and in the power of the Lord Jesus. Take time to ask yourself this question: Is my heart full of a steadfast faith in God's love? If this is not the case, focus on this before you begin to pray. Faith does not come of itself. Consider quietly how impossible it is for God to lie. He is ready with infinite love to give you His blessing. Take some text of Scripture in which God's power, faithfulness, and love are revealed. Apply the words and say, "Yes Lord, I will pray with firm faith in You."

It is a mistake to limit the word "faith" to the forgiveness of sins and to our acceptance as children of God. Faith includes far more. We must have faith in all that God is willing to do for us. We must have faith according to our special needs. Jesus Christ gives grace for each new day, and our faith must reach out according to the needs of the day.

When you enter into the Father's presence and before you begin to pray, ask yourself, "Do I really believe that God is here with me and that the Lord Jesus will help me to pray?" Jesus often taught His disciples how indispensable faith was to true prayer. He will teach us as well.

Lord Jesus, teach me this lesson. Strengthen my faith in Your almighty power. May I see the glory of God, for I ask in Your name, amen.

CONFESSION OF SIN

If we confess our sins to him,
he is faithful and just to forgive us
and to cleanse us from every wrong.
I JOHN 1:9

Too often the confession of sin is superficial and neglected. Few Christians realize how absolutely necessary confession is. An honest confession of sin gives power to live a life of victory over sin. We need to confess with a sincere heart every sin that may be a hindrance in our Christian lives.

Listen to what David says: "I confessed all my sins to you and stopped trying to hide them. I said to myself, 'I will confess my rebellion to the Lord.' And you forgave me! All my guilt is gone. . . . For you are my hiding place; you protect me from trouble. You surround me with songs of victory" (Psalm 32:5, 7). David speaks of a time when he was unwilling to confess his sin. "When I refused to confess my sin, I was weak and miserable" (verse 3). But when he had confessed his sin, a wonderful change came.

Confession means not only that I confess my sin with shame and repentance, but that I turn it over to God, trusting Him to take it away. Such confession implies that I am unable to get rid of my guilt unless, by an act of faith, I trust God to deliver me. This deliverance means that I know my sins are forgiven and that Christ undertakes to cleanse me from the sin and keep me from its power.

Dear Father, I commit myself to confess
each sin, knowing that You will grant forgiveness
and give me deliverance. Thank You that my bur-
den of sin is taken by Jesus. In His name, amen.

THE HOLY SPIRIT

"He will bring me glory by revealing to you
whatever he receives from me."
JOHN 16:14

The last night that He was with His disciples, Jesus promised to send the Holy Spirit as a Comforter. Although His bodily presence was removed, they would realize His presence in them and with them in a wonderful way. The Holy Spirit of God would reveal Christ in their hearts so that they would experience His presence with them continually. The Spirit would glorify Christ and would reveal to them the glorified Christ in love and power.

Do not fail to understand, to believe, and to experience this wonderful truth. Doing the Lord's work is not a duty performed in one's own strength. No, that is impossible. It is the Holy Spirit alone who will teach us to love Him sincerely.

God must have entire possession of us. He claims our whole heart and life. He will give us the strength to have fellowship with Christ, to keep His commandments, and to abide in His love. Once we have grasped this truth, we will begin to feel our deep dependence on the Holy Spirit and ask the Father to send Him in power into our hearts.

Lord, teach me to love the Word, to meditate on it and to keep it. Reveal the love of Christ to me that I may love Him with a pure heart. In His name, amen.

PRAYER AND FASTING

Jesus told them. . . "But this kind of demon
won't leave unless you have prayed and fasted."
MATTHEW 17:21

J esus teaches us that a life of faith requires both prayer
and fasting. Prayer grasps the power of heaven, fasting loosens the hold on earthly pleasure.

Jesus Himself fasted to get strength to resist the
devil. He taught His disciples that fasting should be in
secret, and the Father would reward it openly. Abstinence
from food, or moderation in taking it, helps to focus on
communication with God.

Let's remember that abstinence, moderation, and self-
denial are a help to the spiritual life. After having eaten a
hearty meal, one does not feel much desire to pray. To willingly sacrifice our own pleasure or enjoyment will help to
focus our minds more fully on God and His priorities. The
very practice needed in overcoming our own desires will
give us strength to take hold of God in prayer.

Our lack of discipline in prayer comes from our
fleshly desire of comfort and ease. "Those who belong to
Christ Jesus have nailed the passions and desires of their
sinful nature to his cross and crucified them there"
(Galatians 5:24). Prayer is not easy work. For the real
practice of prayer—taking hold of God and having communion and fellowship with Him—it is necessary that our
selfish desires be sacrificed.

Isn't it worth the trouble to deny ourselves daily in
order to meet the holy God and receive His blessings?

Heavenly Father, help me to joyfully give up
earthly pleasures and the desires of the flesh so
that my prayers may be more powerful and effec-
tive. In Jesus' name, amen.

CHRIST IN ME

*Examine yourselves to see if your faith
is really genuine.*
2 CORINTHIANS 13:5

C hrist is in me. What a difference it would make if we could take time every morning to focus on the thought: Christ is in me.

Christ made it clear to His disciples. The Spirit would teach them: "When I am raised to life again, you will know that I am in my Father, and you are in me, and I am in you" (John 14:20). Through the power of God we who believe were crucified with Christ and raised again with Him. As a result, Christ is in us! Through faith in God's Word, the Christian accepts it.

Paul expresses this thought in the prayer of Ephesians 3:16: "I pray that from his glorious, unlimited resources he will give you mighty inner strength through his Holy Spirit." Notice that it is not the ordinary gift of grace, but a special revelation of the riches of His love that Christ may dwell in your heart by faith. Have you been able to grasp that?

Paul said: "I fall to my knees and pray to the Father" (Ephesians 3:14). That is the only way to obtain the blessing. Take time in prayer in His presence to realize: "Christ dwells in me." Even in the midst of your daily schedule, look upon your heart as the dwelling place of the Son of God. Then Christ's words: "Those who remain in me, and I in them, will produce much fruit" (John 15:5) will become your daily experience.

Father, today as I come quietly before You in secret, help me to experience the wonderful reality of Christ in me. Amen.

CHRIST IS ALL

Christ is all that matters,
and he lives in all of us.
COLOSSIANS 3:11

Christ is all—in the eternal council of God, in the redemption on the cross, as King on the throne in heaven and on earth. In the salvation of sinners, in the building up of Christ's Body, in the care for individuals—Christ is all. Every hour and every day this knowledge provides comfort and strength to the child of God.

You feel too weak, too unworthy, too untrustworthy. But if you will only accept the Lord Jesus in childlike faith, you have a guide who will supply all your need. Believe the word of our Savior in Matthew 28:20: "And be sure of this: I am with you always," and you will experience His presence each day.

However cold and dull your feelings may be, however sinful you are, meet the Lord Jesus in secret and He will reveal Himself to you. Tell Him how miserable you really are, and then trust Him to help and sustain you.

Each day as you spend time in His presence, let this thought be with you: Christ is all. Make it your goal: Christ is all—to teach me to pray, to strengthen my faith, to give me the assurance of His love, to give me direct access to the Father, to make me strong for the schedule of the day.

Lord Jesus Christ, You are all I need. Teach me to abide in Your love so I will have the assurance that You dwell in my heart. May I know the love that passes knowledge. Praise God! You, Christ, are my all in all! Amen.

THE LOVE OF GOD

God is love,
and all who live in love live in God,
and God lives in them.
1 JOHN 4:16

The love of God—what an unfathomable mystery! Jesus said: "Only God is good" (Matthew 19:17). The glory of God in heaven is that He wills to do all that is good. That includes the two meanings of the word: good—all that is right and perfect; good—all that makes happy.

The God who wills nothing but good is a God of love. He does not demand His own way. He does not live for Himself but pours out His love on all living creatures. All created things share in this love so that they may be satisfied with that which is good.

A characteristic of love is that it "does not demand its own way" (1 Corinthians 13:5). It finds happiness in giving to others. It sacrifices itself wholly for others. God offered Himself to mankind in love in the person of His Son, and the Son offered Himself upon the cross to bring that love to men and women. The everlasting love with which the Father loved the Son is the same love with which the Son loves us.

The love of God to His Son, the love of the Son to us, the love with which we love the Son, the love with which we love each other and try to love all men—all is the same eternal, incomprehensible, almighty love of God. Love is the power of the Godhead in the Father, Son, and Holy Spirit.

God of love, thank You for loving me the way You do. It is beyond my understanding. I praise You for Your love. Amen.

As God Forgives

"And forgive us our sins—just as
we forgive those who have sinned against us."
Luke 11:4

The forgiveness of sins is the one great gift that sets the sinner free. Forgiveness gives us boldness toward God and is the source of our salvation. The forgiveness of sins gives us a reason to be thankful every day of our lives.

As we walk with God in the assurance of sins forgiven, He desires that we should live as those who have been freely forgiven. We can only prove our sincerity by forgiving those who have offended us as willingly as God has forgiven us.

In the Lord's Prayer we are taught to pray: "Forgive us our sins, just as we have forgiven those who have sinned against us." Then at the end: "But if you refuse to forgive others, your Father will not forgive your sins" (Matthew 6:12, 15).

In Matthew 18:21, we have the question of Peter: "Lord, how often should I forgive someone who sins against me?" Our Lord answered, "Seventy times seven!"

Then follows the parable of the servant whose lord forgave him his debt but who would not show compassion on his fellow servant. His lord asked, "Shouldn't you have mercy on your fellow servant just as I had mercy on you?" So the servant, was sent to prison. The Lord warns us, "That's what my heavenly Father will do to you if you refuse to forgive your brothers and sisters in your heart" (Matthew 18:33, 35).

Lord, as I need Your forgiveness each day, so let me be ready to forgive my brother. In Jesus' name, amen.

PRAY FOR LOVE

And may the Lord make your love grow
and overflow to each other and to everyone else,
just as our love overflows toward you.
1 THESSALONIANS 3:12

Paul gives us a powerful prayer in this text: that the Lord would make them abound in love toward each other, so that their hearts would be without blame. Without love, true holiness was impossible. Let us use this prayer often.

In 2 Thessalonians 3:5 we read: "May the Lord bring you into an ever deeper understanding of the love of God." This is what the Lord Jesus will do for us. As the apostle makes love the chief thing, let us do the same.

"I want you to know how much I have agonized for you. . . . My goal is that [you] will be encouraged and knit together by strong ties of love. I want [you] to have full confidence because [you] have complete understanding of God's secret plan, which is Christ Himself" (Colossians 2:1–2).

Paul considers love indispensable for growth in the knowledge of God. God's love can only be experienced when Christians are knit together in love and live for others, not only for themselves.

Take time to meditate on these prayers of Paul. As the sun freely gives its light to the grass that it may grow, so God is more willing to give His love to us. As you pray and ponder these words, you will gain a strong assurance of what God is able to do for you. He will make you to abound in love and strengthen you to live before Him in holiness and love for others.

"Lord, grant me a heart of love. May my love
"overflow more and more, and. . . keep on growing
in your knowledge and understanding." Amen.

LIKE CHRIST

"Do as I have done to you."
JOHN 13:15

The love of Christ is the basis not only of our salvation but also of our daily life and conduct. Jesus clearly says, "Do as I have done to you." The love of Christ is my only hope of salvation. Walking in that love is the way to enjoy that salvation.

"We should please others. If we do what helps them, we will build them up in the Lord. . . . So accept each other just as Christ has accepted you; then God will be glorified" (Romans 15:2, 7). God will work within us to accept each other just as Christ has accepted us.

"Follow God's example in everything you do, because you are his dear children. Live a life filled with love for others, following the example of Christ, who loved you and gave himself as a sacrifice to take away your sins" (Ephesians 5:1–2). Paul reminds us that love is everything. Christ loved us so much, He died on the cross so we could be God's dear children. It follows that we should walk in love. Those who keep close to Christ will walk in love.

"Since God chose you to be the holy people whom he loves, you must clothe yourselves with tenderhearted mercy. . . . You must make allowance for each other's faults and forgive the person who offends you. Remember, the Lord forgave you, so you must forgive others. And the most important piece of clothing you must wear is love. Love is what binds us all together in perfect harmony" (Colossians 3:12–14).

Oh God, Father of love, Father of Christ, our Father, will You indeed strengthen us each day to love one another in Christ, even as He loved us! Amen.

TIME FOR PRAYER

Yet no one calls on your name
or pleads with you for mercy.
ISAIAH 64:7

At a ministerial meeting, the superintendent of a large district said: "I rise in the morning and have half an hour with God. I am occupied all day with numerous engagements. Not many minutes elapse without my breathing a prayer for guidance. After work I speak to God of the day's work. But I know little of the intense prayer of which Scripture speaks."

There are earnest Christians who have just enough prayer to maintain their spiritual position but not enough to grow spiritually. Seeking to fight off temptation is a defensive attitude rather than an assertive one which reaches for higher attainment. The scriptural teaching to cry out day and night in prayer must, to some degree, become our experience if we are to be intercessors.

A man said to me, "I see the importance of much prayer, and yet my life hardly allows time for it. Am I to give up? How can I accomplish what I desire?"

I admitted that the difficulty was universal and quoted a Dutch proverb: "What is heaviest must weigh heaviest." The most important must have the first place. The law of God is unchangeable. In our communication with heaven, we only get as we give. Unless we are willing to pay the price—to sacrifice time and attention and seemingly necessary tasks for the sake of the heavenly gifts—we cannot expect much power from heaven in our work.

Father, I see that I am not alone. If others with time pressure can learn to pray as they should, then I can also. Teach me to pray. In Jesus' name, amen.

HEALTH FOR THE SOUL

He was amazed to see that
no one intervened to help the oppressed.
ISAIAH 59:16

How can our lack of prayer be transformed into a blessing? How can it be changed into the path where evil may be conquered? How can our relationship with the Father become one of continual prayer?

We must begin by going back to God's Word to study the place God intends for prayer to have in the life of His child. A fresh understanding of what prayer is and what our prayers can be will free us from our wrong attitudes concerning the absolute necessity of continual prayer. We need insight into how reasonable this divine appointment is.

We need to be convinced of how it fits in with God's love and our happiness. Then we will be freed from the false impression of prayer being an arbitrary demand. We will yield to it and rejoice in it as the only way for the blessing of heaven to come to earth. It will no longer be a task and burden of self-effort and strain. As simple as breathing is in the physical life, so will praying be in the Christian life that is led by the Spirit.

Our failure in the prayer life is a result of our failure in the Spirit life. Any thought of praying more and of praying effectively will be in vain unless we are brought into closer intimacy with our Lord. His life of prayer on earth and of intercession in heaven is breathed into us in the measure that our surrender and our faith allow.

Lord God, enable us for the work of intercession which is the greatest need of the Church and the world today. Amen.

A LIVING CONNECTION

Jesus Christ is the same yesterday, today, and forever.
HEBREWS 13:8

In the history of the Church, two great truths stand out. Where there is much prayer, there will be much of the Spirit; where there is much of the Spirit, there will be ever-increasing prayer. When the Spirit is given in answer to prayer, it stimulates more prayer to prepare for a fuller revelation and communication of His divine power and grace. If prayer was the power by which the early Church flourished and triumphed, is it not the one need of the Church today?

Perhaps these should be considered axioms in our ministries:

1. Heaven is still as full of stores of spiritual blessing as it was then.

2. God still delights to give the Holy Spirit to those who ask Him.

3. Our life and work are still as dependent on the direct impartation of divine power as they were in Pentecostal times.

4. Prayer is still the appointed means for drawing down these heavenly blessings in power on ourselves and those around us.

5. God still seeks for men and women who will, with all their other work of ministering, specially give themselves to persevering prayer.

Lord God, make all these truths live in us. May we not rest until they have mastered us and our whole heart is so filled with them that we count the practice of intercession as our highest privilege. In Jesus' name, amen.

PERSISTENCY THAT PREVAILS

"Don't bother me.
The door is locked for the night, and we are all in bed.
I can't help you this time."
LUKE 11:7

The faith of the host in Luke 11 met a sudden and un-expected obstacle—the rich friend refuses to hear: "I can't help you this time." The loving heart had not counted on this disappointment and cannot accept it. The asker presses his threefold plea: Here is my needy friend; you have abundance, I am your friend. Then he refuses to accept a denial. The love that opened his house at mid-night and then left it to seek help must conquer.

Here is the central lesson of the parable: In our inter-cession we may find that there is difficulty and delay in the answer. It may be as if God says, "I can't help you this time." It is not easy to hold fast our confidence that He will hear and then to continue to persevere in full assurance that we shall have what we ask. Even so, this is what God desires from us. He highly prizes our con-fidence in Him, which is essentially the highest honor the creature can render the Creator. He will therefore do anything to train us in the exercise of this trust in Him. Blessed the man who is not staggered by God's delay or silence or apparent refusal, but is strong in faith giving glory to God. Such faith perseveres, importunately if need be, and cannot fail to inherit the blessing.

Father, when You delay in answering my
prayers, I sometimes think the worst and wonder
if You have determined not to listen to my
request. Help me to be persistent and to never
fail to trust You. In Jesus' name, amen.

CERTAINTY OF A RICH REWARD

"But I tell you this—though he won't do it as a friend,
if you keep knocking long enough,
he will get up and give you what you want
so his reputation won't be damaged."
LUKE 11:8

O h that we might believe in the certainty of an abundant answer! Would that all who find it difficult to pray much would focus on the reward and in faith trust the divine assurance that their prayer cannot be in vain.

If we will only believe in God and His faithfulness, intercession will become the very first thing we do when we seek blessing for others. It will be the very last thing for which we cannot find time. It will become a thing of joy and hope because we recognize that we are sowing seed that will bring forth fruit a hundredfold.

Time spent in prayer will yield more than time given to work. Only prayer gives work its worth and its success. Prayer opens the way for God Himself to do His work in and through us. Let our primary ministry as God's messengers be intercession; in it we secure the presence and power of God.

" 'Suppose you went to a friend's house at midnight, wanting to borrow three loaves of bread' " (Luke 11:5). This friend is none other than our God. In the darkness of midnight, in the greatest need, when we have to say of those we care for, "I have nothing for him to eat," let us remember that we have a rich Friend in heaven.

Father, Creator of the universe, thank You
for Your generosity to Your followers. Thank You
for the promise of answered prayer. May we trust
without wavering. Amen.

A STRENGTHENING PRAYER LIFE

"Listen to me! You can pray for anything,
and if you believe, you will have it."
MARK 11:24

The consequence of sin that makes it impossible for God to give at once is a barrier on God's side as well as ours. The attempt to break through the power of sin is what makes the striving and the conflict of prayer such a reality.

Throughout history people have prayed with a sense that there were difficulties in the heavenly world to overcome. They pleaded with God for the removal of the unknown obstacles. In that persevering supplication, they were brought into a state of brokenness, of entire resignation to Him, and of faith. Then the hindrances in themselves and in heaven were both overcome. As God prevails over us, we prevail with God.

One cause of our neglecting prayer is that there appears to be something arbitrary in the call to such continued prayer. This apparent difficulty is a divine necessity and is the source of unspeakable blessing.

Try to understand how the call to perseverance and the difficulty that it throws in our way is one of our greatest privileges. In the very difficulty and delay will the true blessedness of the heavenly life be found. There we learn how little we delight in fellowship with God and how little we have of living faith in Him. There we learn to trust Him fully and without reservation. There we truly come to know Him.

Though it is very difficult, Lord, I ask that
You will continue to teach me through the delays
and difficulties associated with prayer. In Jesus'
name, amen.

DIFFICULT PRAYER

He prayed more fervently,
and he was in such agony of spirit that his sweat
fell to the ground like great drops of blood.
LUKE 22:44

Have you ever noticed how much difficulties play a part in our life? They call forth our power as nothing else can. They strengthen character.

All nature has been so arranged by God that nothing is found without work and effort. Education is developing and disciplining the mind by new difficulties which the student must overcome. The moment a lesson has become easy, the student is advanced to one that is more difficult. It is in confronting and mastering difficulties that our highest accomplishments are found.

It is the same in our relationship with God. Imagine what the result would be if the child of God had only to kneel down, ask, get, and go away. Loss to the spiritual life would result. Through difficulties we discover how little we have of God's Holy Spirit. There we learn our own weakness and yield to the Holy Spirit to pray in us. There we take our place in Christ Jesus and abide in Him as our only plea with the Father. There our own will and strength are crucified. There we rise in Christ to newness of life. Praise God for the need and the difficulty of persistent prayer as one of His choice means of grace.

Think what Jesus owed to the difficulties in His path. He persevered in prayer in Gethsemane and the prince of this world with all his temptation was overcome.

Lord Jesus, in persevering prayer may I walk
with You and learn of crucifixion. May I share in
the fellowship of Your cross. Amen.

THE MARK OF
A PRAYING CHRISTIAN

The earnest prayer of a righteous person
has great power and wonderful results.
JAMES 5:16

Remember the marks of the true intercessor: a sense of the need of those without Christ, a Christlike love, an awareness of personal inadequacy, faith in the power of prayer, courage to persevere in spite of refusal, and the assurance of an abundant reward. These are the qualities that change a Christian into an intercessor.

These are the elements that mark the Christian life with beauty and health. They fit a person for being a blessing in the world. These are the attitudes that call forth the heroic virtues of the life of faith.

Nothing shows more nobility of character than the spirit of enterprise and daring which battles major difficulties and conquers. So should we who are Christians be able to face the difficulties that we meet in prayer. As we "work" and "strive" in prayer, the renewed will asserts its royal right to claim what it will in the name of Christ.

We should fight our way through to the place where we can find liberty for the captive and salvation for the perishing. The blessings which the world needs must be called down from heaven in persevering, believing prayer.

Our work is often insignificant due to our little prayer. Let us change our method and make unceasing prayer be the proof that we look to God for everything and that we believe that He hears us.

Holy Spirit, answer our prayer. Take complete possession of us to do Your work through us. Amen.

THE LIFE THAT CAN PRAY

*"I chose you, I appointed you to go
and produce fruit that will last,
so that the Father will give you whatever
you ask for, using my name."*
JOHN 15:16

O ur power in prayer depends upon our life. When our life is right, we will know how to pray in a way pleasing to God, and our prayer will be answered. "If you stay joined to me," our Lord says, "you may ask any request you like, and it will be granted" (John 15:7). According to James, it is the prayer of a righteous man that "has great power and wonderful results" (James 5:16).

In the parable of the vine, Jesus taught that the healthy, vigorous Christian may ask what he or she wishes and will receive it. He says, "If you stay joined to me and my words remain in you, you may ask any request you like, and it will be granted." Again he says, "You didn't choose me. I chose you. I appointed you to go and produce fruit that will last, so that the Father will give you whatever you ask for, using my name" (John 15:16).

What life must one lead to bear fruit? What must a person be in order to pray with results? What must one do to receive what he or she asks? The answer is simple. Live as a branch depending on the vine for strength. The source of power in prayer is the vine. If we are branches, abiding in Christ, the vine, He will supply the power. If we trust the vine, then we can ask what we wish and it will be granted.

Lord Jesus, may we live more and more as branches of You, the Vine. May much fruit result from our prayers. Amen.

PRUNING FOR PRAYER

*"He prunes the branches that do bear fruit
so they will produce even more."*
JOHN 15:2

The more aware we become of our inability to pray in power, the more we are helped to press on toward the secret of power in prayer. Jesus said, "I am the true vine, and my Father is the gardener" (John 15:1). We not only have Jesus Himself. We have the Father, as the husbandman, watching over our growth and fruit-bearing. It is not left to our faith. God Himself will see to it that the branch is what it should be. He will enable us to bring forth just the fruit we were appointed to bear. "He prunes the branches that do bear fruit so they will produce even more." The Father seeks more fruit. More fruit is what the Father Himself will provide.

Of all fruit-bearing plants, there is none that produces so much wild wood as the vine. Every year it must be pruned. It is like this for the Christian. The branch that desires to abide in Christ and bring forth fruit must yield itself to divine cleansing.

The gardener cuts away true, honest wood that the branch has produced. It must be pruned because it draws away the strength of the vine and hinders the flow of the juice to the grape. The luxuriant growth of wood must be cast away so that abundant life may be seen in the cluster.

There are things in you that sap away your interest and strength. They must be pruned. Pruning results in a life that can pray.

I am grateful, Lord, that You are a loving gardener. I trust myself into Your loving care and ask You to prune me that I may bear much fruit. Amen.

IS PRAYERLESSNESS SIN?

*I will not remain with you any longer
unless you destroy the things among you that
were set apart for destruction.*
JOSHUA 7:12

If we are to deal effectively with the lack of prayer, we must ask, "Is it sin?" Jesus is Savior from sin. When we experience sin, we can know the power that saves from sin. The life that can pray effectively is one that knows deliverance from the power of sin. But is prayerlessness sin?

Experiencing the presence of God is the great privilege of God's people and their power against the enemy. Throughout Scripture the central promise is that God is with us. The wholehearted person lives consciously in God's presence.

Defeat and failure are due to the loss of God's presence. This was true at Ai. God brought His people into Canaan with the promise of victory. With the defeat at Ai, Joshua knew that the cause must be the withdrawal of God's power. God had not fought for them.

In the Christian life, defeat is a sign of the loss of God's presence. If we apply this to our failure in prayer, we see that it is because we are not in full fellowship with God.

The loss of God's presence is due to sin. He has given Himself wholly to His people. He delights in being with them. He never withdraws Himself unless they compel Him to do so by sin.

*I am grateful, Lord, for Your presence. May I
not lose it through the sin of prayerlessness.
Where I fail, forgive me and restore me to close
fellowship. In Jesus' name, amen.*

THE DISCIPLES:
THEIR DIVINE MISSION

Suddenly, Jesus was standing there among them!
"Peace be with you," he said.
JOHN 20:19

The disciples had received Mary's message of Christ's resurrection. Late in the evening the men from Emmaus told how He had been made known to them. Now their hearts were prepared for when Jesus stood in their midst and said, "Peace be unto you" and showed them His hands and His feet. "They were filled with joy when they saw their Lord! He spoke to them again and said, 'Peace be with you. As the Father has sent me, so I send you' " (John 20:20–21).

With Mary, He revealed Himself to her fervent love that could not rest without Him. With the men at Emmaus, it was their constraining prayer that received the revelation. Here He meets the willing servants whom He had trained for His service. He changes their fear into boldness to carry out the work the Father had entrusted to them.

For this divine work they needed nothing less than Divine power. He breathed upon them the resurrection life and fulfilled the promise He gave: "For I will live again, and you will, too" (John 14:19).

The word is spoken to us, too: "As the Father has sent me, so I send you. . . . Receive the Holy Spirit" (John 20:21–22).

Heavenly Father, with a heart of love and constraining prayer, I ask for Your presence. May Your presence and power be mine for Your service today. Amen.

THE POWER OF OBEDIENCE

"And the one who sent me is with me—
he has not deserted me.
For I always do those things that are pleasing to him."
JOHN 8:29

In these words Christ tells us what His life with the Father was. At the same time, He reveals the law of all communion with God—simple obedience.

In John 14 He says three times: "If you love me, obey my commandments" (verses 15, 21, and 23). Also in chapter 15: "When you obey me, you remain in my love, just as I obey my Father and remain in his love. . . . You are my friends if you obey me" (verses 10 and 14).

Obedience is the proof and the exercise of the love of God in our hearts. It comes from love and leads to love. It assures us that we are abiding in the love of Christ. It seals our claim to be called the friends of Christ. So it is not only a proof of love but of faith, too. It assures us that, "We will receive whatever we request because we obey him and do the things that please him" (1 John 3:22).

Obedience enables us to abide in His love and gives us the full experience of His unbroken presence. It is to the obedient that the word comes: "And be sure of this: I am with you always" (Matthew 28:20) and to whom all the fullness of its meaning will be revealed.

Father, You have said, "I will write [my laws] on their hearts" (Jeremiah 31:33). "I will put my Spirit in you so you will obey my laws and do whatever I command" (Ezekiel 36:27). May my full obedience to Your Word bring the joy of Your abiding presence. In Your Son's name, amen.

THE POWER OF INTERCESSION

*Then we can spend our time in prayer
and preaching and teaching the word.*
ACTS 6:4

In his travels throughout Asia, Dr. Mott was moved by the need for united prayer in the missionary endeavor. He writes: "There is no better way to serve the deepest interest of the Church than by multiplying the number of real intercessors and by focusing their prayers on those situations which demand the almighty working of the Spirit of God. Far more important than any service we can give to missions is that of helping to release the superhuman energy of prayer. Immeasurably more important than any other work is the linking of all we do to the fountain of divine life and energy. The Christian world not only has a right to expect mission leaders to set forth the facts and methods of the work, but also a larger discovery of superhuman resources and spiritual power."

And where is there a greater need of focusing the united intercession of Christians than on the great army of missionaries? They tell of their need for the presence and the power of God's Spirit in their life and work. They long for the experience of the abiding presence and power of Christ every day. They need it; they have a right to it. Shouldn't we become a part of that great army that pleads with God for the power which is so absolutely necessary for effective work?

Dear Father, it is clear that the effectiveness of Your work relies on the releasing of Your power through prayer. May we continue steadfastly in prayer until Your power is sent forth. Amen.

THE POWER OF TIME

My times are in Your hand.
PSALM 31:15 NKJV

My time is in Your hand! It belongs to You. You alone have a right to command it. I yield it wholly and gladly to Your disposal. "What mighty power time can exert if wholly given up to God! Time is lord of all things. The history of the world is proof of how, slowly but surely, time has made man what he is today. All around us we see the proofs, such as the growth of a child to manhood. It is under the law of time and its inconceivable power that we spend our lives.

This is especially true in communion with God—all on the one condition: that we have sufficient time with God. Yet we often confess the weakness of our spiritual life and the inadequate results of our work. This is due to the failure to take time for daily communion with God.

What can be the cause of this sad confession? Nothing less than a lack of faith in the God-given assurance that time spent alone with Him will indeed bring into our lives the power to do His work.

Through prayer, submit your timetable to the inspection of Christ and His Holy Spirit. A new life will be yours if you fully believe and put into daily practice the word: "My time is in Your hand."

Dear God, I confess how often I allow my schedule to be filled with the unimportant, and I don't give enough time to You. Today I yield it wholly and gladly to Your disposal. In Jesus' name, amen.

THE TRIAL AND TRIUMPH OF FAITH

"Anything is possible if a person believes."
MARK 9:23

What a glorious promise: "Anything is possible if a person believes." Yet it is the greatness of this promise that constitutes the trial of faith. At first we do not really believe its truth. But when we have grasped it, then comes the real trial in the thought: Such a faith is utterly beyond my reach. But what constitutes the trial of faith soon becomes its triumph.

When the father of the child heard Christ say, "Anything is possible if a person believes," he felt that this would only cast him into deeper despair. How could his faith be able to work the miracle? Yet we read that the father believed that Jesus not only had the power to heal his child, but also the power to inspire him with the needed faith. The impression Christ generated upon him produced the second miracle, that he could have such great faith. And with tears he cried, "I do believe, but help me not to doubt!" The very greatness of faith's trial was the greatness of faith's triumph.

Through our trials we can experience the abiding presence of Him who speaks to us now: "I am with you always." Let us wait upon God in prayer until we can say in faith, "I do believe."

Dear Father, I am entirely dependent on the power of Christ to enable me to claim all Your promises. May my faith triumph as I declare: "I can do everything with the help of Christ who gives me the strength I need" (Philippians 4:13). In the name of Jesus, amen.

THE MISSIONARY'S LIFE

You yourselves are our witnesses—
and so is God—that we were pure and honest
and faultless toward all of you believers.
1 THESSALONIANS 2:10

Paul more than once appeals to what his converts had seen of his own life. So he says: "We can say with confidence and a clear conscience that we have been honest and sincere in all our dealings. We have depended on God's grace, not on our own earthly wisdom. That is how we have acted toward everyone, and especially toward you" (2 Corinthians 1:12). Christ had taught His disciples as much by His life as by His teaching. Paul also sought to be a living witness to the truth of all that he had preached about Christ.

Paul appeals to the example of his own life throughout his writings. In Philippians 4:9 Paul writes: "Keep putting into practice all you learned from me and heard from me and saw me doing, and the God of peace will be with you."

Let us believe that when Paul said, "I myself no longer live, but Christ lives in me" (Galatians 2:20), he spoke of an actual abiding of Christ in him. Christ was working in him to do all that was well-pleasing to the Father. While in prayer, do not rest until you can say, "The Christ of Paul is my Christ. His empowerment is mine, too."

Father, too often my actions hide the Christ whom I should be revealing. Help me to manifest the character of Christ so others can see and understand His message. In Jesus' name, amen.

THE FRUIT OF THE SPIRIT

But when the Holy Spirit controls our lives,
he will produce this kind of fruit in us:
love, joy, peace. . . .
GALATIANS 5:22–23

The first two lessons on prayer are: We must ask the Father to give us the Spirit anew every morning, and then ask the Spirit to teach us and help us. Here is a third lesson: Commit to memory today's text.

Christians often think they only need to ask God to teach them to pray and that He will do it at once. This is not always the case. When we ask Him to teach us, it is important that we first of all surrender ourselves to the working of the Spirit. This surrender consists in naming before Him the fruit of the Spirit, with the earnest prayer to be filled with this fruit.

Think of the first three—*love, joy, peace*—the three chief characteristics of a strong faith life. Love: to God, to believers, and to all man. Joy: the proof of the provision for every need of courage and faith for all the work we have to do. Peace: the blessed state of undisturbed rest and security in which God can keep our hearts and minds.

In His last talk with the disciples, Christ used these words: "Remain in his love. . .so that you will be filled with my joy" (John 15:10–11). "I am leaving you with a gift—peace of mind and heart" (John 14:27).

Holy Spirit, please make Your fruit reach perfection in me. Then may I be able to pray as I should, always asking more and more of the Heavenly Father, knowing He will answer. In Jesus' name, amen.

LED BY THE SPIRIT

For all who are led by the Spirit of God
are children of God.
ROMANS 8:14

Let us think about four other fruits of the Spirit: patience, kindness, goodness, and gentleness. These all denote attributes of God. They will reach maturity in us as we pray for the working of the Holy Spirit.

Patience—In the Old Testament God's patience was praised. All Scripture bears witness to the patience God had for sinful man. This attribute of the Spirit will enable us to exercise divine patience with all sin and wrong so that sinners may be saved.

Kindness—We read wonderful things in the Psalms about God's kindness. God can enable us to show this same mercy toward those around us.

Goodness—"Only God is truly good" (Luke 18:19). All goodness comes from God, and He gives to His children as each heart asks and desires. This goodness is manifested in sympathy and love to all in need.

Gentleness—It was chiefly in God's Son that the divine gentleness was shown. The Holy Spirit longs to impart gentleness to our hearts.

These four attributes of God may be brought to maturity in our hearts by the Holy Spirit so that we may be like Jesus.

Lord Jesus, through Your Spirit, teach me to
be patient, kind, good, and gentle so that people
may be attracted to You. In Your name, amen.

TIME

"Couldn't you stay awake
and watch with me even one hour?"
MATTHEW 26:40

Every minute spent in prayer is valuable. If ten minutes is all the time you can give, see what you can do in that time. Most people can spare more time. If you will only persevere from day to day, time will come of its own accord.

Is it possible that Christians can say that they cannot afford to spend a quarter or half an hour alone with God and His Word? When a friend comes to see us, or we have to attend an important meeting, or there is anything to our advantage or pleasure, we find time easily enough.

But God has a right to us and longs for us to spend time with Him, and we find no time for fellowship with Him. Even God's own servants are so occupied with their own work that they find little time for that which is all important—waiting on God to receive power from on high.

Dear child of God, let us never say, "I have no time for God." Let the Holy Spirit teach us that the most important and profitable time of the whole day is the time we spend alone with God. Communion with God through His Word and prayer is as indispensable to us as the food we eat and the air we breathe. Whatever else is left undone, God has the first and foremost right to our time.

Lord God, forgive me when my attitude
toward prayer is casual. In the name of Your Son,
Jesus, I ask for a heart that is ever growing in its
desire to spend time with You. Amen.

THE WORD OF GOD

For the word of God is full of living power.
HEBREWS 4:12

I find it a great help to use God's Word in my prayers. If the Holy Spirit impresses a certain text upon my mind, I plead the promise. This habit increases our faith, reminds us of God's promises, and brings us into harmony with God's will. We learn to pray according to God's will and understand that we can only expect an answer when our prayers are in accordance with that will. (1 John 5:14)

Prayer is like fire. Fire can only burn brightly if it is supplied with good fuel. That fuel is God's Word, which must be studied carefully and prayerfully. His Word must be taken into the heart and lived out in the life.

We are all familiar with the characteristics of a seed— a small grain in which the life-power of a whole tree slumbers. If it is placed in the soil, it will grow and increase and become a large tree.

Each word or promise of God is a seed containing a divine life in it. If I carry it in my heart by faith, love it and meditate on it, it will slowly, surely spring up and bring forth the fruit of righteousness.

The Holy Spirit uses both the Word and prayer. Prayer is the expression of our human need and desire. The Holy Spirit teaches us to use the Word as a guide to what God will do for us.

Dear Lord, thank You for Your Word and for the role it has in my prayer life. Help me to apply in prayer what I learn from it. In Jesus' name, amen.

THE SPIRIT GLORIFIES CHRIST

"He will bring me glory by
revealing to you whatever he receives from me."
JOHN 16:14

To understand and experience the work of the Holy Spirit, you must try to grasp the relationship of the Holy Spirit to the Lord Jesus. Our Lord said that the Spirit would come as a comforter to the disciples. The Spirit would reveal Him in their hearts. The disciples held on to that promise. They would not miss their Lord but have Him with them always. This made them pray earnestly for the Holy Spirit for they longed to have Jesus with them always.

This is the meaning of our text—"He will bring me glory by revealing to you whatever he receives from me." Where there is an earnest desire for the glory of Jesus in the heart of the believer, the Holy Spirit will preserve the presence of Jesus in our hearts. We must not weary ourselves with striving after God's presence. We must quietly endeavor to abide in fellowship with Christ, to love Him and keep His commandments, and to do everything in the name of Jesus. Then, we will be able to count upon the secret but powerful working of the Spirit within us.

If our thoughts are always occupied with the Lord Jesus—His love, His joy, His peace—then the Holy Spirit will graciously bring the fruit of the Spirit to ripeness within us.

Lord Jesus, teach me this mysterious union
between You and the Holy Spirit. May the Spirit
so work in me so that I will know Your presence
in everything I do. Amen.

WALK IN THE SPIRIT

Live according to your new life in the Holy Spirit. . . .
If we are living now by the Holy Spirit, let us follow the
Holy Spirit's leading in every part of our lives.
GALATIANS 5:16, 25

The Christian in his daily walk must follow the leading of the Spirit. That will be the sign of a spiritual person who serves God in the Spirit and does not trust in his own abilities.

The Spirit is not needed just when we pray or just for our work for God's kingdom. God gives us His Spirit to be in us the whole day. We need Him most in the middle of our daily work because there the world has such power to lead us away from God. We need to ask the Father every morning for a fresh renewal of His Spirit. During the course of the day, let us remind ourselves that the Spirit is with us.

Paul says, "Now, just as you accepted Christ Jesus as your Lord, you must continue to live in obedience to him" (Colossians 2:6). Again, "Put on the Lord Jesus Christ" (Romans 13:14 NKJV). Just as we put on a coat when we go out, so we must put on the Lord Jesus. We must show by our conduct that Christ lives in us and that we walk by the Spirit.

"Live according to your new life in the Holy Spirit. Then you won't be doing what your sinful nature craves" (Galatians 5:16). If we are not under the guidance of the Holy Spirit, we will do things in our own strength. The Spirit is given to teach us that we may walk by the Spirit at all times.

Thank You, God, for this divine leader Who
gives us daily renewal from heaven and enables us
to walk and to abide in Christ. In Your name, amen.

Rivers of Living Water

"If you believe in me, come and drink!
For the Scriptures declare that
rivers of living water will flow out from within."
John 7:38

Jesus, in His conversation with the Samaritan woman, said: "The water I give them takes away thirst altogether. It becomes a perpetual spring within them, giving them eternal life" (John 4:14). In John 7:38 the promise is even greater: rivers of living waters flowing from Him, bringing life and blessing to others. John says that this refers to the Holy Spirit who would come when Christ had been glorified.

What do we need in order to experience the rivers of living water? Just one thing: the inner connection to Christ —the unreserved surrender to fellowship with Him. We have the firm assurance that His Spirit will work in us what we cannot do. We need a faith that rejoices in the divine power and love. We need a faith that depends on Him day by day to grant us grace that living water may flow out from us.

If the water from a reservoir is to flow into a house all day, one thing is necessary: The connection must be perfect. Then the water passes through the pipe of its own accord. So the connection between us and Christ must be uninterrupted. Our faith must accept Christ and depend on Him to sustain the new life.

Lord God, I rejoice that Jesus Christ gives us the Holy Spirit! Thank You for the assurance that the Holy Spirit is within me as a fountain of blessing. I pray in Jesus' name, amen.

ALL THE DAY—EVERY DAY

I will bless you every day.
PSALM 145:2

It is a step forward in the Christian life when you seek to have fellowship with God in His Word each day without fail. Perseverance will be crowned with success if you are really sincere. The experience may be somewhat as follows:

When you wake up in the morning, God will be your first thought. Set apart a time for prayer and resolve to give God time to hear requests and to reveal Himself. You may share all your desires with God and expect an answer.

Later on in the day, even if only for a few minutes, take time to keep up the fellowship with God. And again in the evening take time to reflect on the day's work and, with confession of sin, receive the assurance of forgiveness. Then commit yourself anew to God and His service.

Gradually you will get an insight into what is lacking in life and will be ready for uninterrupted fellowship with God through the Holy Spirit. You will gain the assurance through faith that the Holy Spirit, the Lord Jesus, and the Father Himself will give His presence and help all through the day.

Remember that you only need to live life one day at a time. You don't have to worry about tomorrow but rest in the assurance that He who has led you today will be even closer tomorrow.

Lord God, grant me the perseverance to spend time each day with You in Your Word and in prayer. In Jesus' name, amen.

WHAT TO PRAY

Pray for each other.
JAMES 5:16

Scripture calls us to pray for many things: for all Christians, for all men and women, for all in government, and for all who are in adversity. It tells us to pray for sending missionaries, for those in the ministry of the gospel, for believers who have fallen into sin, for those in our own circle of friends. The Church is now much larger than when the New Testament was written. The number of ministries and workers is much greater. The needs of the Church and the world are so much better known that we must take time to see where prayer is needed and to what our heart is most drawn.

The scriptural calls to prayer demand a large heart, taking in all saints, and all men and women, and all needs. An attempt will be made these next days to indicate what the chief subjects are that need prayer and that ought to interest every Christian.

It may be difficult to pray for such large spheres as are sometimes mentioned. Where one subject appears of more special interest or more urgent than another, spend some time day after day to pray about that. If you really give time to intercession and the spirit of believing intercession is cultivated, the object is accomplished. While the heart must be enlarged at times to take in all, the more pointed and definite our prayer can be, the better.

Father, may this adventure of learning more about what to pray for result in a renewed relationship with You and with those for whom I pray. Amen.

THE SPIRIT OF PRAYER

"I will pour out a spirit of grace and prayer."
ZECHARIAH 12:10

The evangelization of the world depends first of all upon a revival of prayer. It is needed more than personal witness or missionaries. Deep down at the bottom of our spiritless life is the need for the forgotten secret of the persistent, worldwide prayer.

Every child of God has the Holy Spirit in him to pray. God waits to give you the spirit in full measure.

Pray in the Spirit as Paul taught us: "Pray at all times and on every occasion in the power of the Holy Spirit" (Ephesians 6:18). Jude also wrote, "Continue to pray as you are directed by the Holy Spirit" (Jude 20).

On His resurrection day, our Lord gave His disciples the Holy Spirit to enable them to wait for the full outpouring on the day of Pentecost. It is only as we acknowledge and yield to the power of the Spirit already in us that we can pray for His full manifestation.

Father, Your love is so endless, so mighty, so willing to take possession of me. Let that love have full sway in my heart. Draw me to Yourself that I will continue in prayer and delight in fellowship with You until You take full control. Fill me with the desire and the power to pray for this world. Amen.

CONVINCING THE WORLD OF SIN

"I will send [the Counselor] to you.
And when he comes,
he will convince the world of its sin."
JOHN 16:7–8

The one object of Christ's coming was to take away sin. The first work of the Spirit in the world is conviction of sin. Without that, no real conversion is possible. Pray that the gospel may be preached in such power that men may see that they have rejected and crucified Christ and come to know His saving grace.

Pray most earnestly for a mighty power of conviction of sin wherever the gospel is preached.

Take hold of God's strength when you pray. Read what Isaiah wrote. "These enemies will be spared only if they surrender and beg for peace and protection" (Isaiah 27:5). "Yet no one calls on your name or pleads with you for mercy" (Isaiah 64:7). Paul adds, "Fan into flames the spiritual gift God gave you" (2 Timothy 1:6).

First, take hold of God's strength. God is a Spirit. I cannot take hold of Him except by the Spirit. Take hold of God's strength and hold on until He has done for you what He has promised.

Second, by the Holy Spirit's power in you, fan the flame of intercession in you. Give your whole heart and will to it.

Dear Jesus, in love and concern for the lost, I ask that You stir up a mighty power of conviction of sin wherever the gospel is preached. For Your name's sake, amen.

KINGS AND RULERS

Pray for all people. As you make your requests,
plead for God's mercy upon them, and give thanks.
1 TIMOTHY 2:1

Our text is an example of real faith in the power of prayer! A few weak and despised Christians are to influence the mighty Roman emperors and help secure peace and quietness. Prayer is a power that is honored by God in His rule of the world. Let us pray for our country and its rulers, for all the rulers of the world, for rulers in cities or districts in which we are interested. When God's people unite, they can count upon their prayer affecting the unseen world more than they know.

Prayer is an incense before God. "Then another angel with a gold incense burner came and stood at the altar. And a great quantity of incense was given to him to mix with the prayers of God's people, to be offered on the gold altar before the throne. The smoke of the incense, mixed with the prayers of the saints, ascended up to God from the altar where the angel had poured them out. Then the angel filled the incense burner with fire from the altar and threw it down upon the earth; and thunder crashed, lightning flashed, and there was a terrible earthquake" (Revelation 8:3–5).

The same incense burner brings the prayers of the saints before God and throws fire upon the earth. The prayers that go up to heaven have their share in the history of this earth. Be assured that your prayers enter God's presence.

May those in authority over us, Lord, know
the wisdom of Your Spirit and govern in right-
eousness. In Jesus' name, amen.

THE UNREACHED

"See, my people will return from far away, . . .
from as far south as Egypt."
ISAIAH 49:12

Will the unreached come to Christ? Does God have such a plan? "Let Egypt come with gifts of precious metals; let Ethiopia bow in submission to God" (Psalm 68:31). "I, the Lord, will bring all to pass at the right time" (Isaiah 60:22).

Pray for those who are yet without the Word. China with her hundreds of millions without Christ; India with its millions; millions each year living in darkness. If Christ gave His life for them, you can give yourself up to intercede for them.

If you have not started to intercede, begin now. God's Spirit will draw you on. Persevere, however hesitant you are. Ask God to give you some country or people group to pray for. Can anything be nobler than to do as Christ did—to give your life for the unreached?

Pray with confident expectation of an answer. "Ask me and I will tell you some remarkable secrets about what is going to happen here" (Jeremiah 33:3). "This is what the Sovereign Lord says: I am ready to hear Israel's prayers. . .and I am ready to grant them their requests" (Ezekiel 36:37). Both texts refer to promises definitely made, but their fulfillment would depend upon prayer.

Father, I pray for God's fulfillment of Your
promises to Your Son and the Church. Bring the
unreached to Yourself. I ask in Jesus' name,
amen.

THE LOCAL CHURCH

"Beginning in Jerusalem."
LUKE 24:47

Most of us are connected with some church congregation—a community of believers. They are to us the part of Christ's body with which we come into the most direct contact. They have a special claim on our intercession. Let it be a settled matter between God and you that you are to intercede on their behalf. Pray for the minister and all leaders and workers. Pray for the believers according to their needs. Pray for conversions. Pray for the power of the Spirit to manifest itself. Join with others in specific prayer. Let intercession be a definite work, carried on as systematically as preaching or Bible studies. And pray, expecting an answer.

Pray continually. Read the Scriptures. "Watchmen. . . will pray to the Lord day and night. . . . Take no rest, all you who pray" (Isaiah 62:6). "His chosen people who plead with him day and night" (Luke 18:7). "Night and day we pray earnestly for you" (1 Thessalonians 3:10). "But a woman who is a true widow, one who is truly alone in this world, has placed her hope in God. Night and day she asks God for help and spends much time in prayer" (1 Timothy 5:5).

When the glory of God, and the love of Christ, and the needs of others are revealed to us, the fire of this unceasing intercession will begin to burn in us for those who are near and those who are far away.

Holy Spirit, please come upon my church with the spirit of revival. Fill our pastor so that we may see Your power work in and through him. In Jesus' name, amen.

CHRIST AS KING

*"I assure you that some of you standing here
right now will not die before you see
the Kingdom of God arrive in great power!"*
MARK 9:1

Christ said that it would be in the lifetime of some who heard Him that the kingdom would come in power. That meant that when He, as King, had ascended the throne of the Father, the kingdom would be revealed in the hearts of His disciples. In the kingdom of heaven, God's will is always being done. Christ's disciples would do His will even as it was done in heaven.

We can see in the King the mark of what a kingdom is. Christ was now on the throne of the Father. On earth its power is seen in the lives of those it rules. Only in them the united Body can be seen. Jesus Himself taught how close the relationship would be. "On that day you will realize that I am in my Father, and you are in Me, and I am in you."

This is our first lesson. We must know that Christ rules in our hearts as King. We must know that in His power we are able to accomplish all that He wants us to do. Our whole life is to be devoted to our King and the service of His kingdom. This comes only through consistent daily prayer.

Lord Jesus Christ, I hunger for daily fellowship with You in prayer. May my prayer life be a continuous and unbroken exercise. I rejoice in You, my King, and know that in You I can be more than conqueror. In Your name, amen.

THE HOLY SPIRIT

"You will be baptized with the Holy Spirit. . . .
But when the Holy Spirit has come upon you,
you will receive power."
ACTS 1:5, 8

A mark of the Church is the power for service through the Holy Spirit. Since the time of Adam's fall when he lost the spirit God had breathed into him, God's Spirit had worked with people and worked in some with power. But He had never been able to find His permanent home in them.

It was only when Christ had come, had broken the power of sin by His death, and had won a new life for men in the resurrection, that the Spirit of God could come and take possession of the whole heart.

Nothing less than this could be the power—in the disciples and in us—by which sin could be overcome and prisoners set free. This Spirit is the Holy Spirit. In the Old Testament He was called the Spirit of God. But in the cross of Christ the holiness of God was magnified, and Christ has purified us that we might be pure like Him.

He is the Spirit of the Son. On earth, He led the Son, and Christ yielded Himself implicitly to the leading of the Spirit, even to the crucifixion. The Spirit now reveals Christ in us as our life and our strength, for a perfect obedience.

Father, it is always amazing to us that we should be temples of the Holy Spirit. Make us worthy of such a gift and may You always be free to pray through us. In the name of our Lord, amen.

MY WITNESSES

"You. . .will tell people about me everywhere."
ACTS 1:8

Another mark of Christ's Church: His servants are to be witnesses to Him, testifying of His love, of His power to redeem, of His abiding presence, and of His power to work in them.

This is the only weapon that the King allows His redeemed ones to use. Without claiming authority, power, wisdom, or eloquence, without influence or position, each one is called by words and action to be living proof of what Jesus can do.

This is the only weapon they are to use in conquering men and bringing them to the feet of Christ. This is what the first disciples did. It was in this power that those who were scattered abroad by persecution went out preaching in the name of Jesus. And a multitude believed. They had no commission from the apostles; they had no special gifts or training, but out of the fullness of the heart they spoke of Jesus Christ.

This is the secret of a flourishing Church: every believer a witness for Jesus. And this is the cause of the weakness of the Church: so few willing to testify daily that Jesus is Lord.

What a call to prayer!

Lord, teach us the blessedness of so knowing Jesus and the power of His love that we may find our highest joy in witnessing to who He is and what He has done for us. In Jesus' name, amen.

THE EARTH FILLED
WITH HIS GLORY

Bless his glorious name forever!
Let the whole earth be filled with his glory.
PSALM 72:19

What a prospect—this earth, now under the power of the evil one, renewed and filled with the glory of God. Though it is hard to believe, it surely will come to pass; God's Word is the pledge of it. God's Son, by His blood and death, conquered the power of sin. The power of God is working out His purpose and the whole earth will be filled with His glory.

But it is a difficult work. It is two thousand years since Christ ascended to the throne, and yet hundreds of millions have never learned the name of Jesus. Of the rest, there are millions called by His name, yet they don't even know Him. This work of bringing the knowledge of Christ to every creature has been entrusted to a Church that thinks little of its responsibility and of the consequence of its neglect. Will the work ever be done? God's power and faithfulness are pledges that one day we shall see it—the whole earth filled with the glory of God.

What a wonderful prayer! For it is a prayer: "Let the whole earth be filled with his glory. Amen and Amen!" Every believer is called to this prayer. How wonderful to know that true prayer will indeed be answered! What joy to seek God's face and, with confidence, pray with perseverance until the earth is full of His glory!

Father, when I have driven the last nail and laid the last brick of my life structure, may I hear You say, "Well done." In Jesus' name, amen.

UNITY IS STRENGTH

After this prayer. . .
they were all filled with the Holy Spirit. . . .
All the believers were of one heart and mind.
ACTS 4:31–32

We see the power of union everywhere in nature. How tiny is a drop of rain as it falls? But when many drops are united in one stream, the power quickly becomes irresistible. Such was the power of Pentecost. And our prayer can be like that if we unite all our forces in pleading the promise of the Father.

Because of the many mountains in Natal, the streams often flow down with great force. The Zulus join hands when they want to pass through a stream. The leader has a strong stick in the right hand and gives his left hand to some strong man who comes behind him. And so they form a chain and help each other cross the current. When God's people reach out their hands to each other in the spirit of prayer, there will be power to resist the terrible influence that the world can exert. In that unity God's children will have power to triumph with God.

Christ's followers stayed ten days in the upper room until they truly had become one heart. When the Spirit of God descended, He not only filled each individual but took possession of the whole group as the Body of Christ. It is in the fellowship of loving and believing prayer that our hearts can be melted into one. Then we will become strong to believe and to accept what God has promised us.

We are especially thankful, Lord, for the millions of Christians who share in the work of Your kingdom. May we never forget to hold them up in prayer. We love them, Lord. Amen.

PRAYER AND SACRIFICE

I want you to know how much I have agonized for you.
COLOSSIANS 2:1

People who undertake a great venture have to prepare themselves and direct all their abilities to that end. Likewise, we as Christians need to prepare ourselves to pray just as God's Word tells us to love God: "with all your heart, all your soul, all your strength, and all your mind" (Luke 10:27). This is the law of the kingdom. Prayer needs sacrifice of comfort, of time, of self. Sacrifice is the secret of powerful prayer.

Christ Jesus, the great Intercessor, was an example of sacrifice in prayer. In Gethsemane, "he offered prayers and pleadings, with a loud cry and tears, to the one who could deliver him out of death" (Hebrews 5:7). Prayer *is* sacrifice. David said: "Accept my prayer as incense offered to you, and my upraised hands as an evening offering [sacrifice]" (Psalm 141:2).

Our prayer receives its worth from being rooted in the sacrifice of Jesus Christ. As He gave up everything in His prayer, "Your will be done," our attitude must always be the offering up of everything to God and His service.

When we are reluctant to make the needful sacrifice in waiting upon God, we lack power in our prayer. Christ—the Christ we trust in, the Christ that lives in us—offered Himself as a sacrifice to God. It is as this spirit lives and rules in us that we will receive power to pray the earnest prayer that accomplishes much.

Father, as Jesus took time to pray, may I learn from Him that my time belongs to You. Help me to learn the meaning of dedicated time to You. Amen.

ONE WITH ALL BELIEVERS

"I in them and you in me,
all being perfected into one.
Then the world will know that you sent me
and will understand that you love them
as much as you love me."
JOHN 17:23

The Lord Jesus entrusted these words to us so that we would make them the object of our persistent intercession. Only that would enable us to carry out the last command which He gave: that we should love our brothers and sisters in Christ as He loved us so that our joy would be full.

Our churches today are not always marked by a fervent, affectionate love for all the saints of whatever name or denomination. As a part of our daily fellowship with God, let us pray "that we may be one."

It would be simple if once we connected the words "our Father" with all the children of God throughout the world. Each time we used the words we would only have to expand this little word "our" into all the largeness of God's Father-love. Just as we say "Father" with the thought of our love to Him, we can say "our" with the childlike affection for all the saints whoever and wherever they be. The prayer that "we may be one" would then bring joy and strength, a deeper bond of fellowship with Christ Jesus and all His saints, and an offering of sweet savor to the Father of love.

Thank You, Lord, for all my brothers and sisters who have come by the way of the cross! They are Yours and they are mine. May our fellowship grow as we kneel together. Amen.

ABSOLUTE DEPENDENCE

"Yes, I am the vine; you are the branches. . . .
For apart from me you could do nothing."
JOHN 15:5

The Christian life is a life of absolute dependence. At Hampton Court, there was a vine that sometimes bore a couple thousand clusters of grapes. People were amazed at its productivity. Later the secret was discovered. Not too far from Hampton Court flows the River Thames. The vine had stretched its roots hundreds of yards under the ground until it came to the riverbed. There, in all the nutrients of the river bottom, it found rich nourishment and moisture. The roots drew the sap all that way to the branches.

The vine had the work to do. The branches simply had to depend upon the vine and received what it gave.

That is exactly what Christ desires you to understand. Christ desires that in all your work, the very foundation should be the simple acceptance that Christ must care for all.

As you depend on Him, He supplies your needs by sending down the Holy Spirit. Jesus wants you to be dependent as you serve Him. Day by day, hour by hour, in everything you do, simply abide before Him. Live in the total helplessness of one who can do nothing.

Absolute dependence upon God is the secret of power in work. You and I have nothing unless we receive it from Jesus.

Heavenly Father, thank You for Your nourishment as I learn to be absolutely dependent. Help me to learn well. In Jesus' name, amen.

OUR TOTAL DEPENDENCE ON GOD

"Why ask me about what is good?"
Jesus replied. "Only God is good."
MATTHEW 19:17

Goodness and virtue in our lives is nothing else but the goodness of God manifesting itself in us. Goodness can only belong to God. It is essential to Him and inseparable from Him. All that is glorious and happy in our spirits is only the glory and blessedness of God dwelling in us. The relationship of unalterable dependence on God is the basis of true faith. It is a continual receiving of every degree of goodness and happiness from God alone.

The angels are full of pure love because the glory, the love, and the goodness of God is all that they see and know. Their adoration in spirit and in truth never ceases because they acknowledge their total dependency on God and His centrality to all of creation.

This is the true religion of heaven and this is the one true religion on earth. Nothing in religion can be good unless the power and presence of God really is living and working in it. Mankind must have all its religious goodness wholly and solely from God's immediate activity.

Father, thank You for the wonderful relationship to Yourself for which You created us. Thank You even more for the wonderful redemption which restored us to union and communion with Yourself. Enable us to live in Your power, always keeping in our thoughts our total dependence on You. In Jesus' name, amen.

HUMILITY

"If you want to be my follower
you must love me. . .more than your own life."
LUKE 14:26

The gifts of human learning and wisdom often assert themselves in Christians, instead of that entire dependence upon the Holy Spirit of which Christ spoke. Exaltation of self is the consequence. The Church demonstrates the difference between pride in the power of human learning and humility with absolute dependence on the teaching of the Holy Spirit. Without humility we become self-sufficient and cease from persevering in prayer.

Our minds, by the Fall, are self-sufficient and require self-denial. We need to know two things: 1) Our salvation consists of being saved from ourselves or from that which we are by nature; 2) this salvation was given to us in great humility by God, who manifested Himself in human form. The first stipulation of this Savior to fallen man is: "If you want to be my follower you must love me more than. . . your own life." To show that this is only the beginning of man's salvation, Jesus also says: "Let me teach you, because I am humble and gentle, and you will find rest for your souls" (Matthew 11:29).

What a light is here for those who love the light. Self is the whole evil of the fallen nature; self-denial enables us to become a follower of Jesus, our example of humility.

Father, Your act of humility in becoming a
man so that I can be Your child is an amazing
example to me. Teach me Your humility. Help me
to deny myself and to follow You without reserva-
tion. In Jesus' name, amen.

KEY TO THE
TREASURES IN HEAVEN

*Whatever is good and perfect
comes to us from God above.*
JAMES 1:17

We have been sent into the world with an important errand: by prayer to rise out of the vanity of time into the riches of eternity. We have access to all that is great and good and happy and carry within ourselves a key to the treasures of heaven.

God is not an absent God. He is more present in our souls than our own bodies. We are strangers to heaven and without God because we are void of the spirit of prayer. It opens heaven and the kingdom of God within us. A plant living in the best climate is not so sure of its growth as a person whose spirit aspires after all that God wants to give him.

We are the offspring of God. "In him we live and move and exist" (Acts 17:28). The first man had the breath and spirit of God breathed into him. He was in the image and likeness of God because the Holy Trinity had breathed its own nature into him. The spirit breathed into man brought heaven into man.

The lesson that we find here is one of the deepest truths of God's Word. As willing as the sun is to shine its light on the waiting earth, so is the living God waiting to work in the heart of His child.

*Lord, as sure as the sun shines on this earth,
so my God is sending forth His light and His love
into my heart for me to receive and to rejoice in.
Amen.*

THE GOODNESS OF GOD

"For God so loved the world
that he gave his only Son,
so that everyone who believes in him
will not perish but have eternal life."
JOHN 3:16

The goodness of God was the cause of the creation. In all eternity God's only thought or intent has been to communicate good to His creation. As the sun gives the blessings of life, so our holy God pours forth the riches of divine perfection upon everything that has capacity to receive them.

This is the love of God. He is the unchangeable over-flowing fountain of good. He is love itself,—the un-mixed immeasurable love doing nothing but from love giving nothing but gifts of love. He requires nothing of all His creatures but the fruit of that love which brought them into being. Oh, how marvelous is this contemplation of the height and depth of the riches of divine love.

Look at every part of our redemption—from Adam's sin to the resurrection of the dead and you will find nothing but successive mysteries of that first love which created angels and men. All the mysteries of the gospel are proofs of God's desire to make His love triumph over sin and disorder from all nature.

As God's children we need to wait before God in quiet till His light shines on us. Unless we take time enough with God for His light to shine into the depths of our hearts, it is useless for us to expect that His immeasurable love can enter our hearts and fill our lives.

Our Father, teach us to believe in Your love and not to rest until our hearts are filled with it! Amen.

PRAYER:
A STATE OF THE HEART

Everything else is
worthless when compared with
the priceless gain of
knowing Christ Jesus my Lord.
PHILIPPIANS 3:8

Jesus, though He had all wisdom, only gave us a small number of moral teachings. This is because He knew that the desire of our hearts is focused on this world. Nothing can set us right but turning the desire of our hearts to God. Therefore He calls us to a total denial of ourselves and the life of this world. He calls us to a faith in Him as the one who gives a new birth and a new life. He teaches us every reason for renouncing ourselves and for loving our redemption as the greatest joy and desire of our heart.

We see that our will and our heart are everything. True religion is only the religion of the heart. We see that a spirit of longing after the life of this world made us the poor pilgrims on earth that we are. Only the spirit of prayer, or the longing desire of the heart after Christ and God and heaven, breaks our bondage and lifts us out of the miseries of time into the riches of eternity.

When the spirit of prayer is born in us, it is no longer confined to a certain hour but is the continual breathing of the heart after God. The spirit of prayer, as the state of the heart, becomes the governing principle of the soul's life.

Lord Jesus, by Your Holy Spirit, please develop
in me the spirit of prayer. May I learn to pray all
day, every day. In Jesus' name, amen.

THE SPIRIT OF PRAYER

Pray at all times and on every occasion
in the power of the Holy Spirit.
EPHESIANS 6:18

The spirit of the soul is in itself nothing but a spirit breathed from God. He created it for this end only: that the life of God, the nature of God, the working of God might be manifested in it.

The spirit of prayer is stretching with all our desire after the life of God. It is leaving, as far as we can, our own spirit and receiving a Spirit from above to be one life, one love, one spirit with Christ. This prayer is an emptying of ourselves and our own lusts and desires. It is opening ourselves for the light of God to enter into it. It is the prayer in the name of Christ, to which nothing is denied.

The love of God, His never-ceasing desire to enter and dwell in us and give birth to His Spirit in us, waits no longer once the door of our heart opens. Nothing can hinder God's holy union with the soul except the decision of the heart that is turned away from Him. The life of the soul in itself is nothing but a working will. Wherever the will works, there the soul lives, whether it be in God or in the creature.

Dear Father, may I live out the life that You have chosen for me. Help me to reject all of self and to be totally dependent on You for the spirit of prayer. In Jesus' name, amen.

THE POWER OF PRAYER

"If you stay joined to me and my words remain in you,
you may ask any request you like,
and it will be granted!"
JOHN 15:7

B efore Jesus went to heaven, He taught His disciples two great lessons in regard to their relationship to Him in the work they had to do.

The one was that, in heaven, Jesus would have much more power than He had here on earth. He would now use that power through His disciples for the salvation of men.

The other was that without Him they could do nothing. Their first and chief work would therefore be to bring everything they wanted done to Him in prayer. In His farewell discourse, Jesus repeats the promise seven times: "Remain in me, pray in my name." Ask any request you like and it will be granted." You can count on it!

With these truths written in their hearts, He sent the disciples out into the world to accomplish His work. The disciples on earth always looked up to Him in prayer, fully confident that He would hear their prayer. The first and only condition is an unflinching confidence in the power of His promise.

The same condition applies for us today. Close, abiding fellowship with Christ begins with deep dependence and unceasing prayer. It is only then that we can do our work in the full assurance that God has heard our prayer and will be our source of strength.

Heavenly Father, Your Word promises: "Ask any request you like; and it will be granted." Help me to maintain a spirit of prayer and, in faith, claim Your promises as I remain in You. Amen.

CHRIST OUR LIFE

All who receive God's wonderful,
gracious gift of righteousness will live in triumph over
sin and death through this one man, Jesus Christ.
ROMANS 5:17

Paul teaches that faith in Christ as our righteousness is to be followed by faith in Him as our life from the dead. He now asks: "Have you forgotten that when we became Christians and were baptized to become one with Christ Jesus, we died with him?" (Romans 6:3). We are now to consider ourselves as truly "dead to sin and able to live for the glory of God."

The new life in us is an actual participation in and experience of the risen life of Christ. Our death to sin in Christ is also a spiritual reality. It is only when we see how we were one with Christ on the cross in His death and in His resurrection that we will understand that "death no longer has any power over him" (Romans 6:9).This is the true life of faith.

Being in Christ and having Him live His life in us can only come true as the full power of the Holy Spirit is experienced. Paul says in Romans 8:2 that "the power of the life-giving Spirit has freed you through Christ Jesus from the power of sin that leads to death." And he then adds: "that the requirement of the law would be fully accomplished for us who no longer follow our sinful nature but instead follow the Spirit" (Romans 8:4). Through the Spirit we enter into the glorious liberty of the children of God.

Holy God, I count myself dead to sin and
alive in Christ Jesus. Open my eyes to see the
power of Christ living in me. Work in me a life of
holiness and fruitfulness. Amen.

THE INDWELLING CHRIST

I pray that Christ will be more and more at home
in your hearts as you trust in him.
EPHESIANS 3:17

The great privilege that separated Israel from other nations was this: They had God dwelling in their midst. He made His home in the tabernacle and the temple. In the New Testament we see God dwelling in the heart of the believer. Jesus said: "All those who love me will do what I say. My father will love them, and we will come to them and live with them" (John 14:23). Or, as Paul says of himself, "Christ lives in me" (Galatians 2:20).

The gospel is the dispensation of the indwelling Christ. In Ephesians 3:14, 16, and 17, Paul teaches how we can experience this blessing of the Christian life.

1. *"I fall to my knees and pray to the Father." The blessing must come from the Father to the praying believer.*

2. *"I pray that from his glorious, unlimited resources he will give you mighty inner strength through his Holy Spirit.*

3. *"I pray that Christ will be more and more at home in your hearts as you trust in him." It is in the very nature of Christ to desire to live in the heart of faith.*

4. *"May your roots go down deep into the soil of God's marvelous love."*

Prayerfully meditate on what Christ, through the Holy Spirit, has chosen to do. He has chosen to make His home in our hearts!

Dear Lord, May our hearts be a pleasing dwelling place. In Jesus' name, amen.

NOT SINNING

And you know that Jesus came to take away our sins,
for there is no sin in him.
So if we continue to live in him,
we won't sin either.
1 JOHN 3:5–6

In our text John teaches how we can be kept from sinning: "If we continue to live in him, we won't sin either." Though we are sinful by nature, living in the sinless Christ frees us from the power of sin and enables us to live a life pleasing to God. In John 8:29 the Lord Jesus said of the Father: "I always do those things that are pleasing to him." And so John writes here: "Dear friends, if our conscience is clear, we can come to God with bold confidence. And we will receive whatever we request because we obey him and do the things that please him" (1 John 3:21–22).

Let the one who longs to be free from the power of sin take to heart these simple but far-reaching words: "There is no sin in him." He that establishes us in Christ is God. As I seek to live in Him in whom there is no sin, Christ will indeed live out His own perfect life in me in the power of the Holy Spirit. I will then be equipped to do the things that are pleasing in His sight.

By faith claim these words: "If we continue to live in him, we won't sin either." God the Almighty has pledged to make this promise a reality.

Dear Father, the life I live in Your Son frees
me from the power of sin. As I live in Him help
me to claim and live the promise: "If we continue
to live in him, we won't sin either." In the perfect
name of Jesus, amen.

PRAYER TO BE HOLY

Christ will make your hearts strong, blameless,
and holy when you stand before God our Father
on that day when our Lord Jesus comes.
1 THESSALONIANS 3:13

This is a prayer for holiness, which is the very nature of God, inseparable from His Being. We are in Christ, who is made of God our sanctification. The Spirit of God is the Spirit of holiness. We have been sanctified in Christ Jesus. The new nature we have from Him has been created in true holiness.

It is as we believe in God, through Christ and the Holy Spirit working in us, that the inflow of the holy life from above is renewed. And as we believe we have the courage and the power to live out that holy life.

Believers, God desires your sanctification. Worship God in His holiness until every thought of God in His glory and grace is connected with the deep conviction that the blessed God wills my holiness. Do not rest until your will has surrendered unconditionally to the will of God and found its true destiny in receiving that divine will and working it out.

When, by God's grace, you will as God wills, when you have accepted God's will for sanctification as your own will, you can count on God working it. God wills it with all the energy of His divine being.

Holy Father, strengthen my heart so that I
will be blameless and holy in Your presence.
Teach me how to live so that I please You. In
Jesus' name, amen.

WHEN TROUBLE COMES

Patient endurance is what you need now,
so you will continue to do God's will.
Then you will receive all that he has promised.
HEBREWS 10:36

The first concern of most Christians in trouble is to be delivered from it. However, perhaps this should not be the primary thing. Our one great desire ought to be that we do not fail in knowing or doing the will or God in anything. This is the secret of strength and true character in the Christian life.

When trials come, though, it is beyond human power to think of and do God's will first. It is indeed something beyond human power but not beyond the power of grace. It is just for this that our Lord Jesus came to earth—to do God's will. He went to the cross with the prayer to God: "Not My will, but Yours be done."

Ask God to renew your spirit and your mind and to show you how He would have you live wholly in His will. Yield yourself to that will in everything you know and do it. Yield yourself to that will in all its divine love and quickening power as it works in you and makes you partaker of its inmost nature. Pray, pray, pray, until you see increasingly in Jesus' life and death the promise and pledge of what God will work in you. Your abiding in Him and your oneness with Him mean nothing less than your being called to do the will of God as He did it.

Dear Lord Jesus, I do not intend to be a quitter but to persevere in living Your way. By Your grace I will overcome. Amen.

APPROACHING GOD IN PRAYER

You love him even though you have never seen him.
Though you do not see him, you trust him;
and. . .are happy with a glorious, inexpressible joy.
1 PETER 1:8

When you pray, begin by thanking God for His unspeakable love which invites you to come to Him and communicate freely with Him.

If your heart is cold and dead, remember that worship is not simply a matter of feeling but has to do first with the will. Raise your heart to God and thank Him for the assurance you have that He looks down on you and will bless you. Through such an act of faith you honor God and draw your soul away from being occupied with itself. Think also of the glorious grace of the Lord Jesus who is willing to teach you to pray and give you the desire to do so. Think, too, of the Holy Spirit who was purposely given to intercede for you in prayer. Five minutes spent this way will strengthen your faith for the work of prayer.

Once more I say, begin with an act of thanksgiving. Praise God for the inner chamber of prayer and His promise of blessing there.

It is a great thing to say, but it is the simple truth: God will make the place a Beth-El (house of God) where His angels shall ascend and descend and where you will cry out, "Yahweh will be my God." He will also make it Peni-El (face of God) where you will see the face of God, as a prince of God (Isra-El), wrestling in overcoming-type prayer. It will become the most blessed place on earth.

Father, thank You for the love You show by inviting me to talk with You. I am overwhelmed with joy to know that You want to listen. Thank You! Amen.

No One to Intercede?

He was amazed to see that no one
intervened to help the oppressed.
So he himself stepped in to save them.
ISAIAH 59:16

To be an intercessor before God for others is greatly needed. But do not attempt it hastily or thoughtlessly, as though you know well enough how to pray. Prayer in our own strength brings no blessing. Take time to present yourself reverently and in quietness before God. Remember His greatness and holiness and love. After receiving God's Word into your heart, begin to pray for your own needs and the needs of others.

One reason why prayer does not bring more joy and blessing is that it is too selfish, and selfishness is the death of prayer. Remember your family, your own church, your own neighborhood, and the extended church. Let your heart be enlarged and remember the concerns of missions and of the Church throughout the whole world. Become an intercessor, and you will experience for the first time the blessedness of prayer as you find that you have something to say to God. He will do things in answer to your prayers which otherwise would not have been done.

Lord, the blessings of Your salvation and righteousness are needed by so many. Pour out Your blessings, Almighty Father, to those needing You. Establish justice and mercy throughout this world. Protect those proclaiming the gospel. May many turn to You. Amen.

INTERCESSORY PRAYER

The Spirit pleads for us believers
in harmony with God's own will.
ROMANS 8:27

After we have humbled ourselves before God in praise and thanksgiving, have received His Word in personal communion with Him, and have made our requests for our own needs, God desires that we continue in prayer as intercessors before Him for the needs of others—to grow in our praying.

Children could ask their father for bread, but full-grown children converse with him about all the interests of his business and other areas of life. Weak children of God pray only for themselves, but persons growing in Christ understand how to consult with God over what must take place in the kingdom. Let your prayer list include the names of those for whom you pray—your minister, and all other ministers, and the different missionary affairs with which you are connected. Thus your prayer time will really become a wonder of God's goodness and a fountain of great joy.

We must confess that we have a nature perfectly adapted to do this work God has called us to do. We have been created in Christ to pray.

We must honor God the Holy Spirit, believe that He is praying within us, and yield to the strength and courage He brings to our praying in His power.

Dear Lord, those who need my prayers
have specific needs. Enable me to see their needs
as You see them and to pray wisely and with Your
compassion. In Jesus' name, amen.

MORNING BY MORNING

Listen to my voice in the morning, Lord.
Each morning I bring my requests to you
and wait expectantly.
PSALM 5:3

Many Christians observe the morning watch, while others speak of it as the quiet hour, the still hour, or the quiet time. All these, whether they think of a whole hour or half an hour or a quarter of an hour, agree with the psalmist.

In speaking of the extreme importance of this daily time of quiet for prayer and meditation on God's Word, a well-known Christian leader has said: "Next to receiving Christ as Savior and claiming the baptism of the Holy Spirit, we know of no act that brings greater good to ourselves or others than the determination to keep the morning watch, and spend the first half hour of the day alone with God."

At first glance this statement appears too strong. The firm determination to keep the morning watch hardly appears sufficiently important to be compared to receiving Christ and the baptism of the Holy Spirit. However, it is true that it is impossible to live our daily Christian life, or maintain a walk in the leading and power of the Holy Spirit, without a daily, close fellowship with God. The morning watch is the key to maintaining a position of total surrender to Christ and the Holy Spirit.

Lord, how I need You today. Whatever I have planned is empty and pointless unless You are pleased with it. Please guide me. Amen.

PRAYER'S UNBROKEN FELLOWSHIP

When Moses came down the mountain. . .
he wasn't aware that his faced glowed because
he had spoken to the Lord face to face.
EXODUS 34:29

Close and continued prayer fellowship with God will in due time leave its mark and be evident to those around us. Just as Moses did not know that his face shone, we ourselves will be unaware of the light of God shining from us. The sense of God's presence in us may often cause others to feel ill at ease in our company. However, true believers will prove by humility and love that they are indeed persons like those around them. And yet there will be the proof that they are people of God who live in an unseen world.

The blessings of communion with God can easily be lost by entering too deeply in communion with people. The spirit of inner prayer must be carried over into a holy watchfulness throughout the day. We do not know at what hour the enemy will come. The continuance of the morning watch can be maintained by quiet self-restraint, by not giving the reins of our lives over to natural impulses.

When the abiding sense of God's presence has become the aim of the morning hour, then with deep humility and in loving conversation with those around us, we will pass on into the day's duties with the continuity of unbroken fellowship.

I will walk with You, Master. There is no
finer joy, no greater security or peace than to be
in Your presence all day long. Amen.

ACCORDING TO GOD'S WILL

*And we can be confident that he will listen to us
whenever we ask him for anything in line with his will.*
1 JOHN 5:14

How can we know if we are praying according to
God's will? That is an intensely practical question
to ask as we take time to pray.

To properly understand 1 John 5:14, we must connect the words "in line with his will" with "ask"—not
merely with "anything." Similarly, connect "he will listen" with "whenever we ask." Not only the thing asked
for but also the disposition and character of the one asking must be in line with God's will. Both the thing asked
for and the spirit of asking must be in harmony with
God's will.

Jesus' teaching continually connected the answer to
prayer with a life that was being lived according to God's
will: trusting, forgiving, merciful, humble, believing,
asking in His name, abiding in His love, observing/keep-
ing His commands, and having His words abiding within. He also said that if they loved Him and kept His commands, then He would pray to the Father for them.
Prayer has power according to the life! A life in line with
God's will can ask according to God's will.

When you live according to God's will, you are spiritually able to discern what to ask for. A life yielded to
and molded by the will of God will know what and how
to pray.

*Father, I long to live a life that is yielded
and molded to Your will. Conform me to Yourself
so that I may learn to pray according to Your
will. Amen.*

OPEN THEIR EYES

Elisha prayed, "O Lord,
open his eyes and let him see!". . .
Elisha prayed,
"O Lord, now open their eyes and let them see."
2 KINGS 6:17, 20

The prayer of Elisha for his servant was answered in a wonderful way. The young man saw the mountain full of chariots of fire and horsemen surrounding Elisha. The heavenly host had been sent by God to protect His servant.

Elisha prayed a second time. The Syrian army was struck with blindness and was led into Samaria. There Elisha prayed for God to open their eyes, and they found themselves hopeless prisoners in the hand of the enemy.

All the powers of the heaven are at our disposal in the service of His kingdom. How little the children of God live in the faith of the heavenly vision—the power of the Holy Spirit, on them, with them, and in them.

The church is unconscious of its weakness to do the work of bringing others to Christ and building up believers for a life of holiness and fruitfulness. Pray that God may open eyes to see the great and fundamental need of the Church: the need for intercession to bring down His blessing.

Our Father, You are so unspeakably willing to give the Holy Spirit in power; hear my humble prayer. As You did for Elisha's servant, open my eyes. In Christ's name, amen.

THE BLESSEDNESS OF
A LIFE OF INTERCESSION

Take no rest, all you who pray.
Give the Lord no rest until he makes Jerusalem
the object of praise throughout the earth.
ISAIAH 62:6–7

What a gift of grace to be allowed to work with God in intercession for the needs of others! What a blessing to mingle my prayers with His! What an honor to have power with God in heaven for those who do not know Christ. What a privilege to bring to Him the Church, individuals, ministers, or missionaries, and plead on their behalf until He entrusts me with the answer! As God's children we are blessed to pray together until victory is gained over difficulties here on earth or over the powers of darkness!

For a long time we may have thought of prayer simply as a means of supplying our needs in life. May God help us to see the place intercession takes in His divine counsel, and in His work for the kingdom. May our hearts really feel that there is no honor or joy on earth at all equal to the unspeakable privilege of waiting upon God and interceding for the blessing He delights to give!

Our Father, let Your life indeed bow down to this earth and fill the hearts of Your children! As the Lord Jesus pours out His love in His unceasing intercession in heaven, let it even be so with us also upon earth—a life of overpowering love and never ending intercession. Amen.

THE PLACE OF PRAYER

They all met together continually for prayer.
ACTS 1:14

C hrist spoke these words before He left the world: "Do not leave Jerusalem until the Father sends you what he promised." "When the Holy Spirit has come upon you, you will receive power." "[You] will tell people about me everywhere—in Jerusalem, throughout Judea, in Samaria, and to the ends of the earth" (Acts 1:4, 8).

Such are the marks of the church of the New Testament. The Church that went out to conquer the world was a Church of united and unceasing prayerfulness, a ministry filled with the Holy Spirit, members serving as witnesses to a living Christ, with a message to every creature on earth.

When Christ had ascended to heaven, the disciples knew what their work was to be: continuing with one accord in prayer and supplication. This gave them power in heaven with God and on earth with men. Their duty was to wait united in prayer for the power of the Holy Spirit for their witness to Christ to the ends of the earth. The Church of Jesus Christ should be a praying, Spirit-filled church and a witnessing church to all the world.

As long as the Church maintained this character, it had power to conquer. Unfortunately, as it came under the influence of the world, it lost much of its supernatural strength and became unfaithful to its worldwide mission.

Lord Jesus, have mercy upon Your church. Give, I pray You, the Spirit of prayer and supplication as of old, that Your Church may prove what power from You rests upon her to win the world to Your feet. Amen.

INTERCESSION FOR LABORERS

"The harvest is so great, but the workers are so few.
So pray to the Lord who is in charge of the harvest;
ask him to send out more workers for his fields."
MATTHEW 9:37–38

The disciples understood little of what these words in Matthew meant. Christ gave them as a seed thought for later use. At Pentecost they must have felt that the ten days of united prayer had brought a special blessing as the fruit of the Spirit's power—workers in the harvest.

Christ was teaching us that however large the field and however few the workers, prayer is the best and the only means for supplying the need. We must not only pray in time of need, but all our activity for God is to be carried on in the spirit of prayer. Prayer for workers for God's harvest must be part of our whole life and effort.

When the China Inland Mission had two hundred missionaries, they felt the urgent need of more workers for unreached districts. After much prayer, they felt the freedom to ask God to give them one hundred additional workers within a year. They continued praying throughout the year. At the end of the time, one hundred men and women and the needed funds had been found.

Christ calls us to united, unceasing prayer. God is faithful, by the power of His Spirit, to supply every need. God hears the prayer of the Church.

Blessed Lord Jesus, teach Your church what it means to live and labor for You in the spirit of unceasing prayerfulness. May our faith rise to the assurance that You will, in a way surpassing all expectations, meet the crying need of a dying world. Amen.

The Grace of Intercession

*Devote yourselves to prayer with an alert mind
and a thankful heart.
Don't forget to pray for us, too.*
Colossians 4:2–3

There is nothing that can bring us nearer to God and lead us deeper into His love than the work of intercession. Nothing gives us a higher experience of God than pouring out our hearts to Him in prayer for men and women. Nothing can so closely connect us to Jesus Christ and give us the experience of His power and Spirit as yielding our lives to the work of bringing redemption into the lives of others. There is nothing in which we will know more of the working of the Holy Spirit than the prayer breathed by Him into our hearts, "Abba, Father."

As we become a living sacrifice before God with the persistent prayer for His abundant blessing, God will be glorified. In intercession, our souls will reach their highest destiny and God's kingdom will come.

As God's children daily pray together that God will make His Church a light to those who are sitting in darkness, we will experience unity and power in the Body of Christ. How little we realize what we are losing in not living in fervent intercession!

Christ lives in heaven to pray—asking the fullness of the Spirit for His people. God delights in nothing as much as in prayer. Believe that the highest blessings of heaven will be given to us as we pray more.

Blessed Father, pour down the Spirit of supplication and intercession on Your people for Jesus Christ's sake. Amen.

Link Between Heaven and Earth

"May your Will be done here on earth,
just as it is in heaven."
Matthew 6:10

When God created heaven and earth, He meant heaven to be the divine pattern to which earth was to be conformed. "As in heaven, so on earth" was to be the law of its existence.

What constitutes the glory of heaven? God is there. Everything lives for His glory. When we think of what this earth has become, with all its sin and misery, with the great majority without any knowledge of the true God, we feel that a miracle is needed if the Word is to be fulfilled: "May your Will be done here on earth, just as it is in heaven."

This can become true through the prayers of God's children. Intercession is to be the great link between heaven and earth. The intercession of the Son, begun upon earth, continued in heaven, and carried on by His people, will bring about the change. As Christ prayed "May your Will be done," so His redeemed ones make His prayer their own and unceasingly ask, "May your Will be done here on earth, just as it is in heaven."

When we, God's children, learn to pray not only for our immediate interests but enlarge our hearts to take in the whole Church and the whole world, then our united supplication will have power with God. Intercession will hasten the day when it will indeed be "on earth, just as it is in heaven"—the whole earth filled with the glory of God.

Our Father in heaven, may Your name be honored. May Your kingdom come soon. May Your will be done here on earth, just as it is in heaven." Amen.

A ROYAL PRIESTHOOD

*Ask me and I will tell you some remarkable secrets
about what is going to happen here.*
JEREMIAH 33:3

As you pray for God's great mercies to be granted,
take with you these thoughts:

(1) The infinite willingness of God to bless. His very
nature is a pledge of it. He delights in mercy. He waits to
be gracious.

(2) Why then is the blessing delayed? In creating man
with a free will and making him a partner in the rule of the
earth, God limited Himself. He made Himself dependent
on what man would do. Man by his prayer would hold the
measure of what God could do in blessing.

(3) Think of how God is hindered and disappointed
when His children seldom pray. The weak Church, the
lack of the power of the Holy Spirit, is all because of the
lack of prayer.

(4) Yet God has blessed—just up to the measure of the
faith and the zeal of His people. If He has thus blessed our
weak prayers, what will He do if we yield ourselves
wholly to a life of intercession?

(5) This is a call to repentance and confession! Our
lack of consecration has held back God's blessing from
the world. He was ready to save, but we were not willing
for the sacrifice of a whole-hearted devotion to Christ
and His service.

*Heavenly Father, we as Your followers are
judged and found guilty. In Your great mercy,
bring us to the place of unceasing prayer that
You desire us to share with Your Son. In His
name, amen.*

GOD WILL HEAR ME

But the Lord still waits for you to come to him
so he can show you his love and compassion. . . .
He will be gracious if you ask for help.
He will respond instantly to the sound of your cries.
ISAIAH 30:18–19

The power of prayer rests in the faith that God hears prayer. In more than one sense this is true. This faith gives us courage to pray. This faith gives us power to prevail with God. The moment I am assured that God hears me too, I feel drawn to pray and to persevere in prayer. I feel strong to claim and to take in faith the answer God gives.

One reason for the lack of prayer is the want of the living, joyous assurance, "God will hear me." If only God's servants would get a vision of the living God waiting to grant their request. If they could see that He longs to bestow all the heavenly gifts of the Spirit they are in need of. Then they would set aside everything and make time and room for this power that could ensure heavenly blessing—the prayer of faith!

When you say in faith, "God will hear me!" nothing can keep you from prayer. You know that what you cannot do on earth can and will be done for you from heaven. Let each one of us bow in stillness before God and wait on Him to reveal Himself as the prayer-hearing God. In His presence the wondrous thoughts gathering round the central truth will unfold themselves to us.

Dear God, I rejoice to know that You hear
when I call. I know that You delight in hearing
and answering prayer. I look forward to spending
time with You each day. Amen.

A Wonderful Certainty

As for me, I look to the Lord for his help.
I wait confidently for God to save me.
MICAH 7:7

God will hear me. What a wonderful certainty! We have God's word for it. We have thousands of witnesses that have found it true. We have experienced it ourselves. The Son of God came from heaven with the message that if we ask, the Father will give. Christ prayed on earth; now He is in heaven interceding for us. God hears prayer—God delights in hearing our prayer. He has allowed His people to be tried so that they are compelled to cry to Him and learn to know Him as the Hearer of prayer.

We should confess with shame how little we have believed this truth. We have failed to receive it into our hearts. Accepting a truth is not enough; the living God must be revealed by it so that our whole life is spent in His presence. We must live with an awareness as clear as in a little child toward its earthly parent—I know for certain my Father hears me.

By experience you know how little an intellectual understanding of truth has profited you. Ask God to reveal Himself to you. If you want to live a different prayer life, bow to worship God in silence each time before you pray. Wait there until you have a deep consciousness of His nearness and His readiness to answer. After that you can begin to pray with the words, "God will hear me!"

Father, I bow before You because You will hear me. I know that when You hear, You answer my prayers. Hear my prayer today and grant my request. In Jesus' name, amen.

THE DESIRE FOR GOD

All night long I search for you.
ISAIAH 26:9

What is the best and most glorious thing that a man needs every day and can do every day? Nothing less than to seek, to know, to love, and to praise God Himself. As glorious as God is, so is the glory which begins to work in the hearts and lives of people who give themselves to live for God.

Have you learned to seek this God, to meet Him, to worship Him, to live for Him and for His glory? It is a great step forward in the life of a Christian when we truly see this and consider fellowship with God every day as the chief end of our lives.

Take the time to ask yourself whether knowing your God and loving Him with your whole heart is the utmost desire of your heart. You can be certain that God greatly desires that you should live in this intimate fellowship with Him. He will, in answer to your prayer, enable you to do so.

Begin today by speaking these words to God in the stillness of your soul: "O God, you are my God; I earnestly search for you. My soul thirsts for you; my whole body longs for you. . . . I follow close behind you" (Psalm 63:1, 8). "[I] search for him with all [my] heart" (Psalm 119:2).

Heavenly Father, I desire to know You more deeply each day. May You incline Your heart unto me as I eagerly anticipate Your presence today. In Jesus' name, amen.

FAITH IN GOD

Jesus said to the disciples,
"Have faith in God."
MARK 11:22

As the eye is the organ by which we see, so faith is the power by which we see the light of God and walk in it.

We were made for God, to seek Him, to find Him, to grow up into His likeness and show forth His glory—in the fullest sense to be His dwelling. And faith is the eye which, turning away from the world and self, looks up to God and sees God reveal Himself.

Without faith it is impossible to please God or to know Him. "Abraham never wavered in believing God's promise. . . . He was absolutely convinced that God was able to do anything he promised" (Romans 4:20–21).

Let our one desire be to take time and be still before God, believing with an unbounded faith in His longing to make Himself known to us. Let us feed on God's Word to make us strong in faith. Let that faith have large thoughts of what God's glory is and of what His power is.

Such faith, exercised and strengthened day by day in secret fellowship with God, will become the habit of our life. It will keep us ever in the enjoyment of His presence and in the experience of His saving power.

Dear Father, You have said that, apart from faith, it is impossible to please You. Make me strong in faith so I may please You and know You more fully each day. I trust You with my very soul. Amen.

ALONE WITH GOD

One day as Jesus was alone, praying. . .
he went higher into the hills alone.
LUKE 9:18, JOHN 6:15

Human beings need to be alone with God. Our fall consisted in our being brought, through the lust of the flesh and the world, under the power of the things visible and temporal. Our restoration through salvation is meant to bring us back to the Father's love and fellowship.

We need to be alone with God, to yield ourselves to the presence and power of His holiness. Christ on earth needed it. He could not live the life of a Son here in the flesh without at times separating Himself entirely from His surroundings and being alone with God. How much more must this be indispensable to us!

Alone with God—that is the secret of true power in prayer. There is no true holiness, no clothing with the Holy Spirit and with power, without being alone daily with God.

When our Lord Jesus gave us the command to pray to our Father in secret, He gave us the promise that the Father would hear such prayers and mightily answer them in our life before others. What a privilege it is to begin every morning with intimate prayer. Let it be the one thing our hearts are set on—seeing, finding, and meeting God alone. The time will come when you will be amazed at the thought that one could suggest five minutes was enough.

Heavenly Father, "Listen to my cry for help, my King and my God, for I will never pray to anyone but you. Listen to my voice in the morning, Lord. Each morning I bring my requests to You and wait expectantly" (Psalm 5:2–3). In the precious name of your Son, Jesus, amen.

HALF AN HOUR SILENCE IN HEAVEN

*There was silence throughout heaven
for about half an hour. . . . Then. . .incense was
given to him to mix with the prayers of God's people.*
REVELATION 8:1, 3

There was silence in heaven for about half an hour—
to bring the prayers of the saints before God. Many
of God's children have also felt the absolute need of
silence and withdrawal from the things of earth for half an
hour—to present their prayers before God. In so doing,
they have been strengthened for their daily work.

How often the complaint is heard that there is no time
for prayer. Yet often the confession is made that, even if
time could be found, one feels unable to spend the time in
real communion with God. Don't think, "I will not know
how to spend the time." Just believe that, if you bow in
silence before God, He will reveal Himself to you.

If you need help, read some passages of Scripture and
let God's Word speak to you. Then bow in deepest humility before God and wait on Him. He will begin to work
within you as you intercede for those whom He has laid
upon your heart. Keep praying, though the time may seem
long. God will surely meet you.

Is it not worth the trouble to take half an hour alone
with God? In heaven itself there was need for half an
hour's silence to present the prayers of the saints before
God. If you persevere, you may find the half-hour that
seems the most difficult may become the most blessed in
your whole life.

*Lord, give me the courage today to be alone with
You for a half-hour. Help me to be silent and wait
for You to reveal Yourself. In Jesus' name, amen.*

FULLY COMMITTED HEART

The eyes of the Lord search the whole earth
in order to strengthen those whose hearts
are fully committed to him.
2 CHRONICLES 16:9

In worldly matters we know how important it is that work should be done with the whole heart. In the spiritual realm, this rule should also hold true. God has promised in Jeremiah 29:13 that, "If you look for me in earnest, you will find me when you seek me."

It is amazing that earnest Christians, who attend to their daily work with all their hearts, are so content to take things easy in the service of God. They do not realize that, if anywhere, they should give themselves to God's service with all the power of their will. In the words of our text we get an insight into the absolute necessity of seeking God with a fully committed heart.

What an encouragement this should be to us to humbly wait on God with an upright heart. We can be assured that His eye will be upon us, and He will show forth His mighty power in us and in our work.

O Christian, have you learned this lesson in your worship of God—to yield yourself each morning with your whole heart to do God's will? Pray each prayer in true wholehearted devotion to Him. In faith expect the power of God to work in you and through you.

Dear Lord, as Your eyes run to and fro throughout the whole earth, may You find me to be one with a pure and committed heart. Show Your mighty power in me. In Jesus' name I ask this, amen.

THE OMNIPOTENCE OF GOD

"I am God Almighty."
GENESIS 17:1

When Abraham heard these words, he fell on his face and God spoke to him. God filled his heart with faith in what He would do for him. O Christian, have you bowed in deep humility before God until you felt that you were in living contact with the Almighty?

Read in the Psalms how the saints of old gloried in God and in His strength.

"The Lord protects me from danger" (Psalm 27:1).

"God remains the strength of my heart" (Psalm 73:26).

Take time to appropriate these words and to adore God as the Almighty One, your strength.

Christ taught us that salvation is the work of God and quite impossible to humans. When the disciples asked: "Then who in the world can be saved?" His answer was: "Humanly speaking, it is impossible. But not with God. Everything is possible with God" (Mark 10:26–27). If we firmly believe this, we will have courage to believe that God is working in us all that is well-pleasing in His sight.

Think how Paul prays for the Ephesians, that through the enlightening of the Spirit, they might "begin to understand the incredible greatness of his power for us who believe him" (Ephesians 1:19). When we fully believe that the mighty power of God is working within us, we can joyfully say, "God is the strength of my life."

Most powerful God, let me not rest until I
can say, "I will love You, O Lord, my strength."
Take complete possession of me and complete Your
work in me by the power of Your name, amen.

THE FEAR OF GOD

Happy are those who fear the Lord.
Yes, happy are those who
delight in doing what he commands.
PSALM 112:1

The fear of God—these words characterize the religion of the Old Testament and the foundation which it laid for the more abundant life of the New Testament. The gift of holy fear should still be the great desire of the child of God today.

Paul more than once gives fear a high place in the Christian life: "Put into action God's saving work in your lives, obeying God with deep reverence and fear" (Philippians 2:12). "Let us work toward complete purity because we fear God" (2 Corinthians 7:1).

It has often been said that the lack of the fear of God is one of the things which most characterizes us today. It is no wonder then that we lack the passion for the reading of God's Word and the worship in His house. We feel the absence of that spirit of continuous prayer which marked the early church. We need texts like the one at the beginning of this reading to impress upon us the need for a deep fear of God, leading to an unceasing prayerfulness.

As we pray, let us earnestly cultivate the fear of God. Then take the words "Happy are those who fear the Lord" into our hearts. Believe that it is one of the essential elements of the life of faith.

Lord God, help us to "Serve the Lord with reverent fear, and rejoice with trembling" (Psalm 2:11). "Let us be thankful and please God by worshiping him with holy fear and awe" (Hebrews 12:28). In Your Son's name, amen.

GOD IS INCOMPREHENSIBLE

We cannot imagine the power of the Almighty,
yet he is so just and merciful
that he does not oppress us.
JOB 37:23

This attribute of God as a Spirit whose being and glory are entirely beyond our comprehension is one we ponder all too little. And yet in the spiritual life it is of the utmost importance to know that, as the heavens are high above the earth, so God's thoughts and ways are infinitely beyond all our thoughts.

With deep humility and holy reverence, we must look up to God. Then with childlike simplicity we must yield ourselves to the teaching of His Holy Spirit. "Oh, what a wonderful God we have! How great are his riches and wisdom and knowledge! How impossible it is for us to understand his decisions and his methods" (Romans 11:33).

Let our hearts respond, "O Lord, O God of gods, how wonderful you are in all your thoughts, and your purposes how deep." The study of what God is ought to fill us with holy awe and the longing to know and honor Him. Just think of these attributes—His Greatness; His Might; His Omnipresence; His Wisdom; His Holiness; His Mercy; His Love. How incomprehensible!

As you worship and pray, begin to grasp the inconceivable glory of this Great Being who is your God and Father. By faith, trust that, in a way passing all understanding, this incomprehensible God will work in your heart and life to know Him more fully.

Dear God, I confess with shame how little I
have sought to know You. I desire to know all
that You choose to reveal of Yourself. Amen.

THE HOLINESS OF GOD

You must be holy because I am holy.
I am the Lord, who makes you holy.
LEVITICUS 11:44–45

In Leviticus Israel had to learn that holiness is the highest and most glorious attribute of God. It also must be the marked characteristic of His people today. Those who desire to truly know God and approach Him in prayer, must desire to be holy as He is holy. The priests who were to have access to God had to be set apart for a life of holiness.

The prophet Isaiah, who was to speak for God, was also set apart for a life of holiness. Listen to Isaiah 6: "I saw the Lord. He was sitting on a lofty throne. . . . In a great chorus [the seraphim] sang, 'Holy, holy, holy is the Lord Almighty!' " (verses 1, 3)—the voice of adoration and reverence. "Then I said, 'My destruction is sealed, for I am a sinful man and a member of a sinful race. Yet I have seen the King, the Lord Almighty!' " (verse 5)— the voice of a broken, contrite heart. "Then one of the seraphim flew over to the altar, and he picked up a burning coal. . . . He touched my lips with it and said, 'See, this coal has touched your lips. Now your guilt is removed, and your sins are forgiven' " (verses 6–7)—the voice of grace and full redemption. Then follows the voice of God: "Whom should I send as a messenger to my people?" And the willing answer is: "Lord, I'll go! Send me" (verse 8).

Child of God, meet with your Father in prayer.

Most Holy God, "Holy, holy, holy is the Lord Almighty." Give me a contrite and humble spirit, so that I might always "worship the Lord in all his holy splendor" (Psalm 96:9). Amen.

THE WORD OF GOD

For the word of God is full of living power.
HEBREWS 4:12

When communing with God, His Word and prayer are both indispensable and should not be separated. In His Word, God speaks to me; in prayer, I speak to God.

The Word teaches me to know the God to whom I pray; it teaches me how He would have me pray. It gives me precious promises to encourage me in prayer. It often gives me wonderful answers to prayer.

The more I pray, the more I feel my need of the Word and rejoice in it. The more I read God's Word, the more I have to pray about and the more power I have in prayer. One great cause of prayerlessness is that we read God's Word too little, or only superficially, or in the light of human wisdom.

It is the Holy Spirit through whom the Word has been spoken, who is also the Spirit of prayer. He will teach me how to receive the Word and how to approach God.

What power and inspiration would be ours if we only took God's Word as from Himself, turning it into prayer and definitely expecting an answer. It is in the intimacy of God's presence and by the Holy Spirit that God's Word will become our delight and our strength.

Dear God, Your Word is indeed full of living power. I anticipate Your blessing as I appropriate Your words: "Oh, the joys of those who. . .day and night. . .think about his law" (Psalm 1:1–2). In Jesus' name, amen.

WAITING UPON GOD

On thee do I wait all the day.
PSALM 25:5 KJV

Waiting upon God—in this expression we find one of the deepest truths of God's Word in regard to the attitude of the soul in its communion with God. We should begin each day with this attitude of the soul.

When waking in the morning, in quiet meditation, in the expression of our ardent longings and desires, in the course of our daily work, in all our striving after obedience and holiness, in all our struggles against sin and self-will—in everything there should be a waiting on God to receive His blessing. See what He will do, allow Him to be the almighty God.

Meditate on these things and they will help you to value the precious promises of God's Word: "Those who wait on the Lord will find new strength. They will fly high on wings like eagles" (Isaiah 40:31). "Wait patiently for the Lord. Be brave and courageous. Yes, wait patiently for the Lord" (Psalm 27:14). In these words we have the secret of heavenly power and joy.

As we exercise absolute dependence upon God, it will become more natural to say: "On you do I wait all the day."

Wait on God—that He will reveal Himself in us; that He may teach us all His will; that He may do to us what He has promised; that in all things He may be the infinite God.

Dear Father, quiet my soul to wait on You. "I wait for the Lord, my soul waits, And in His word do I hope" (Psalm 130:5 NKJV). In Jesus' name, amen.

Inspirational Library

Beautiful purse/pocket-size editions of Christian classics bound in flexible leatherette. These books make thoughtful gifts for everyone on your list, including yourself!

When I'm on My Knees   The highly popular collection of devotional thoughts on prayer, especially for women.
Flexible Leatherette. $4.97

The Bible Promise Book   Over 1,000 promises from God's Word arranged by topic. What does God promise about matters like: Anger, Illness, Jealousy, Love, Money, Old Age, and Mercy? Find out in this book!
Flexible Leatherette. $3.97

Daily Wisdom for Women   A daily devotional for women seeking biblical wisdom to apply to their lives. Scripture taken from the New American Standard Version of the Bible.
Flexible Leatherette. $4.97

My Daily Prayer Journal   Each page is dated and features a Scripture verse and ample room for you to record your thoughts, prayers, and praises. One page for each day of the year.
Flexible Leatherette. $4.97

Available wherever books are sold.
Or order from:

Barbour Publishing, Inc.
P.O. Box 719
Uhrichsville, OH 44683
http://www.barbourbooks.com

If you order by mail, add $2.00 to your order for shipping.
Prices are subject to change without notice.